To the Millers,

Blessed U ♀ ☓

Keep Moving

[signature]

Phil. 4:13

KEEP MOVING FORWARD

My Son's Last Words

Lloyd Byers, D. Min. with Mary Byers

WestBow
PRESS
A DIVISION OF THOMAS NELSON

Author photo on backcover taken by Tec Petaja Photography
www.tecpetajaphoto.com

WestBow Press books may be ordered through booksellers or by contacting:

WestBow Press
A Division of Thomas Nelson
1663 Liberty Drive
Bloomington, IN 47403
www.westbowpress.com
1-(866) 928-1240

ISBN: 978-1-4497-1629-5 (sc)
ISBN: 978-1-4497-1630-1 (dj)
ISBN: 978-1-4497-1628-8 (e)

Library of Congress Control Number: 2011927573

Printed in the United States of America

WestBow Press rev. date: 6/6/2011

I want to dedicate this project to my family.
To my wife, Mary, Josh's mother, who continues to show courage and
strength in the midst of grief. Without her support, encouragement,
and love I could not have accomplished this feat. My love for over
forty years. I love you.
To Milam and Jared, my two sons, Josh's brothers, who have walked
with me as I have grieved in the midst of their own grief. I am forever
grateful to you and proud to be your Dad.

"No, dear brothers and sisters, I have not achieved it, but I
focus on this one thing:
Forgetting the past and looking forward to what lies ahead."
Philippians 3:13 New Living Translation

Portions of the Profits
of this book will be donated
by Joshua's Mission to:
Not Alone

www.notalone.com

Not Alone provides programs, resources and services to warriors and families impacted by combat stress and PTSD through a confidential and anonymous community.

American Gold Star Mothers, Inc.

www.goldstarmoms.com

AGSM, Inc. is an organization of mothers who have lost a son or daughter in the service of our country.

And

The Reversal

www.thereversal.org

A ministry serving artists in the touring community, helping them experience Gospel-driven community, through one-on-one mentoring and focused spiritual care.

For more information about

Joshua's Mission

Josh's life and the latest news

And to book all types of speaking engagements

Visit us on the web at: www.joshuasmission.us

CONTENTS

ENDORSEMENTS:

"This excellent book is a beautiful illustration of a life well lived. The life of this exemplary young man was cut short by ruthless, brutal enemies. I believe every person, especially every American youth, should read these true and inspiring words. Joshua Byers is one of the finest examples of what we need Americans to be.

There are other priceless lessons in Lloyd's excellent writing, my favorite being his discussion on helping others in grief, such as people who have lost loved ones.

This writing will bring you to a new level of finding meaning and direction in your life."

Ross Campbell, M.D. Retired Child Psychiatrist and best selling author of "How to Really Love Your Child" and numerous other books.

"After reading the book I feel as though I know Josh better and look forward to having conversations with him in Heaven. We all think our children are the most special in the world, but Josh really stood out from the crowd. I love how you have woven Josh's last words into a lesson on life. It is a tribute to Josh, but yet it is so much more."

Molly Morel, National President American Gold Star Mothers, Inc. 2010-2011
Proud Gold Star Mom of Captain Brent Morel, KIA Iraq, 2004
www.goldstarmoms.com

"As a friend and West Point classmate of Josh, this book strikes home for me. As a combat veteran and infantry officer, my service in Iraq and Afghanistan was just like his. This book portrays so much about the ideals and sacrifices of a real hero and the struggles of so many of our families at home. It's a true portrayal of life at war, both at home and in combat. Josh's sacrifice will always be honored and I will keep moving forward in his name."

Mike Jones, Executive Director of Not Alone, Inc.
www.notalone.com

FOREWORD

Written by
General Charles C. "Hondo" Campbell
GEN(R), USA

Josh Byers was a loving husband, a devoted son, a beloved brother, a wonderful friend, a splendid Soldier, a steadfast comrade, an unwavering patriot, and a committed Christian.

He was a Soldier who made the ultimate sacrifice. He gave the last full measure of devotion so that others might live their lives as men and women of free choice.

CPT Josh Byers did not go to a distant and alien land seeking glory, dominion, or wealth. He went to Iraq because he believed that all peoples, in all nations, have a right to live in a world free from tyranny.

He willingly put himself in harm's way so that a fledgling democracy might take root; so that others might enjoy political and religious freedom; and so that others might raise their children in a world where hope has replaced despair, generosity has replaced brutality, peace has replaced conflict, and where the future can be brighter than the past.

That Josh would make this sacrifice for others is not at all surprising to those of us who knew Josh and who knew his philosophy on life — a philosophy that "center-pieced" service to others.

As a Soldier and as a leader, Josh was "others-focused". He put "others first" at all times and in all circumstances.

Though a man of considerable achievement, conspicuous ability, and enormous potential, he lived his life in a way that reflected an innate sense of humility. Josh had a "servant's heart" and as such "he esteemed others as more important than himself." Josh exemplified the "Servant Leader" described in Luke, Chapter 22 and Mark, Chapter 10. More than anyone I have ever known, Josh's life was characterized by humble and loving service. Josh lived his life in a way that reflected his understanding that "whoever wants to be great must be a servant and whoever wants to be first must be a slave to all".

As a "Servant-Leader" Josh understood that leaders have special relationships with their followers — and importantly — special responsibilities to them. He understood and took seriously his responsibility to promote growth in the professional, moral, spiritual, and relational aspects in the lives of those he led.

He made an investment in his followers because they were special to him and as a result, became special to them. Repeatedly, in assignment after assignment, what emerged was a powerful bond between the leader and the led. A bond that tied spirits together in mutually caring, productive, and protective relationships. Josh's call for commitment, integrity, dedication, and sacrifice on the part of those he led was honored because Josh was himself committed, honest, dedicated, and willing to sacrifice.

I recall that Josh had a wonderful "sense of humanity". As a Soldier and as a leader he had the "human touch". In an environment of stress, fatigue, hardship, and sacrifice — by his calm and inspired leadership — Josh instilled confidence in his Soldiers that they would endure; succeed; and prevail.

Far more than most, Josh understood that those he led needed a sense of worth, belonging, purpose, and competence — and as a "Servant-Leader" he responded to those needs. The Soldiers that Josh Byers led were without exception proud, team-oriented, mission-focused, and proficient.

Josh had an unshakable belief in Jesus Christ as his Lord and Savior. As a "Christian Soldier", Josh was submissive to God's will. Josh believed that God has a specific plan for each one of us and he believed that each one of us must do our best to determine what God's plan is for us and then to submit to it.

As a "Christian Soldier" Josh was obedient to God's word and trusting in God's design. As a "Christian Soldier" — in his daily living — Josh was "warm, sympathetic, understanding, loving, and forgiving". Josh was an unfailing source of support and encouragement to all those whose lives he touched. He was an absolutely inexhaustible fount of energy, excitement, optimism and hopefulness.

As a "Christian Soldier" Josh's faith allowed him to receive God's most precious gift — the "love of life." That "love of life" enabled him to see in each day the "possibilities" for growth; it enabled him to find in each struggle the strength of renewal; and it enabled him to seek in each person the "face of a friend."

Because of his Christian beliefs, Josh understood that greatness is not found in possession, power, position, or prestige but rather it is discovered in goodness, humility, and character.

Josh taught us a great deal about life by the way he chose to live his life. He taught us that the secret to a full, rich, and abundant life has to do with passion, determination, perseverance, commitment, and selfless service.

He taught us that life is not about having and getting but about being and becoming. He taught us that life is not about taking but about giving. He taught us that happiness does not come from "what" we have in our life but rather "who" we have in our life. And he knew, as a Christian, the "who" in your life needed to include Jesus Christ.

Josh taught us that we are what we are because of our relationships. That we need to build our relationships on caring for each other, being devoted to each other, and loving each other.

By the example of his life, Josh taught us that after "all the battles have been fought" and "all the races have been run", there are only three things that truly matter in this world.

First is Duty — duty to our country; duty to our Army; duty to our assigned missions; duty to our comrades; and duty to our families and communities.

The second is our relationship with others. In Josh's life he had many relationships. He treasured the relationships with his family and friends. But his most treasured relationship was with his wife Kim. Josh recognized and appreciated that he was blessed in his marriage to her. She was his soul mate and life partner. He "delighted" in her because she was an unfailing source of love, support, comfort, joy, happiness, and contentment.

Finally, Josh taught us that the third — and most important thing that matters in life — is our relationship with God. Josh taught us that if we wanted to be happy in this world and inherit the next, then we had to let the love of God flow through us and out to others.

His time with us was far too short but Josh taught us much about living an "others-focused", "God-centered" life. We are indebted to him for having been a conduit of God's love and for having touched our lives in enduring and constructive ways. It is a debt that we can only repay — by serving God and by serving others.

General Charles C. Campbell assumed duties as the Commander, United States Army Forces Command at Fort McPherson, Georgia in January 2007. While the Commander of the Army's largest organization, he was responsible for the oversight, manning training, and equipping of 750,000 Active Duty, Reserve and National Guard Soldiers when mobilized for combat operations.

General Campbell has extensive Combined Arms and Joint command and staff experience. He served as the commander of a Special Operations A-Detachment in Vietnam, an armor battalion in the 3rd Armored Division, a mechanized brigade in the 2nd Infantry Division, and as the Commanding General of the 7th Infantry Division. Prior to moving to Fort McPherson for duty as the Deputy Commander at US Army Forces Command, he was the Commanding General for Eighth Army, Republic of Korea.

General Campbell is currently retired and lives with his wife, Dianne, in Shreveport, Louisiana.

It was 23 July 2003, 0730 hours, 120 degrees, Ar Ramadi, Iraq. It was just 4 months into the war.

Captain Joshua Byers, the Commander of Fox Troop in the 2nd Squadron 3rd ACR (Armored Cavalry Regiment), was leading a convoy that had just left their base camp.

On the other side of the world Josh's parents were boarding a plane in Tokyo, Japan bound for Atlanta, Georgia. Josh's two brothers, Milam and Jared were anticipating their arrival.

It was to be a day of celebration, not only for their mother's 50th birthday but also for Milam and Ashley's engagement just 2 days prior.

Without warning, a blast erupted in the Iraqi desert shaking the ground for miles. It would soon be felt by an unsuspecting family a world away.

One confirmed KIA (killed in action), 2 others critically injured.

A knock at the door, 2 men in Army Class A uniforms. They could only be there for one reason.

A phone call.

A husband, son, brother, friend, commander and soldier had been taken in the blast.

This is our story. This is a hero's story.

INTRODUCTION

No matter who you are or what circumstances you face in today's stressful society, we all have to deal with what life throws our way. We wake up to headlines that always include bad news, face our day with jobs that are difficult, deal with tough relationships in family, and wonder if we will be able to afford the next day's financial challenges.

In the wake of this how do you keep moving forward? Do you feel as though you are going in reverse? Perhaps you really are and it causes frustration like you have never known. We are so confused in our day-to-day living in society. Like a termite in a yo-yo; we just don't know where to turn.

My oldest son of three boys knew where he was going since he was in the seventh grade. In my many years of being a pastor (36 to be exact) and dealing with all kinds of relationships, I have never experienced a young person's determined spirit as I did with Josh. He came home from school one day, in the fall of 1986, and announced to his mom and me that he would serve his country when he graduated from college. He even went further and began researching the Air Force Academy. His determination was inspirational in itself and he never wavered from his destiny.

As I introduce you to this book, it is about his life but more importantly his death. On July 23, 2003, his mom's birthday, Josh was killed instantly by a hidden bomb, Improvised Explosive Device, (IED) as he was riding in the lead vehicle of a convoy between Ar Ramadi and Al Fallujah, Iraq.

It is my desire to convey to the reader what a real hero is made of and to describe a determination that most of us struggle with. It is sad that most of our young people today often know about the statistics of an athlete's record or the latest Hollywood gossip but very few know of or about what real heroes are made of. Our great country was built by men and women of courage, strength, and compassion for their fellow man. Most celebrities are only worried about their looks or income. Thank our Almighty God for those who know, for those who have what it takes to persevere, and for those who are committed to make a real difference in human life, which is, after all, the definition of a hero.

As a parent who has lost a child I cannot even begin to share the kind of hurt I feel. It's like trying to communicate to a deaf person the sound of rushing water over a waterfall. Or trying to describe what fresh plowed dirt on the farm smells like to one who has lost his sense of smell. It can be as difficult to describe to a person blind from birth, a country scene with rolling pastures, woods in the distance, dew sparkling like diamonds on the grass as the sun begins to peek from the east early in the morning. We have hope in the God Josh trusted (whom we also trust) therefore because of our Lord Jesus Christ it becomes bearable in the most difficult periods of grief. The Bible tells us in Philippians 4:13 NKJV, "I can do all things through Christ who strengthens me."

The driver of the Humvee in which Josh was riding shared with me that awful experience moment by moment. He even remembered Josh's exact words as he took his last breath.

"Keep Moving Forward"

It is in the three last words Josh shared that are to be preserved and used as a message for my life. More importantly, I believe it is also a message that he left for you, the reader, for it can change your life. We are all just trying to make it in a world of pain, hatred, and heartache. Josh leaves us with a message that can truly make the difference in your life as you face a world full of contradiction and hurt.

I have known very few real heroes in my lifetime but to have known one who was my son is very humbling. We all need more heroes.

"Where I was born, and when and how I lived is unimportant. It is what I have done and where I have been that should be of interest."
-Georgia O'Keefe

CHAPTER ONE

BORN IN A MINISTER'S HOME

"Is tasteless food eaten without salt, or is there flavor in
the white of an egg?" Job 6:6 NIV

We need more heroes. Heroes help shape our lives. Heroes help clarify our
values. Heroes help define our character. I believe we all need a mentor.
We all need a model to mold our lives after so we can accomplish the
goals we've set. We are all born with the deep desire in our souls to
fulfill a purpose, whatever that looks like individually to each of us. I
have experienced many visitors in my office who share that they have a
little happiness, a little joy, a little peace, but that something is missing
somewhere deep inside their souls. In most cases, I have found that folks
are not finding the purpose that Almighty God has put inside of them,
so they keep running in many directions instead of the right way to really
plant that fulfilled, peaceful feeling one has when one's purpose is being
pursued. I have talked to some who have already retired and still have not
settled in their hearts and souls what has been missing for so many years.
They admittedly share that, even though on the surface it seemed they were
truly happy, they never have had the satisfaction deep in their souls as they
lay down at night of really being fulfilled in their goals for life.

In the Old Testament of God's Word, the Bible, Job was the richest
man in all the East. When God and Satan communicated about what a
great, faithful servant of God Job was, Satan challenged the Lord with
the fact that Job would not be so "great" if he lost all his riches and his
children. Well, he lost all he had including his children and to add insult
to injury, he came down with the terrible malady called "elephantiasis."

The boils and sores all over his body were so painful Job would take a piece of broken pottery to scrape over the heads of the boils to give him a few seconds of relief from the throbbing of the sores as he was sitting in an ash heap. Job's wife, who obviously showed a true lack of faith, told him to curse God and take his life (with a wife like that it would really be tempting). Job's friends told him his real problem was that he was paying for sins he had committed in the past (with friends like those, one does not need any enemies). And Job looked up and said, "Does it taste good to eat something without salt or is there any taste in the white of an egg?" Job was saying, "My life is like that, and there is something missing in my life." Job had become proud at this point and turned *from* God, in a sense, without turning *away* from God.

Our heavenly Father created us for one reason and one reason only — and that reason was fellowship. God wanted us to fellowship with Him and to love Him. As a human race we were made to walk with God until the sin of pride and rebellion happened in the Garden of Eden and perfection was no more. I believe the very reason many people today feel like something is missing in their lives is not the fact that they did not accomplish making a fortune or reaching the upper level of power and prestige; it is that most do not fellowship with God in an intimate way. I know because, as a pastor, I hear many say "but I come to church" or "I serve on a church committee" or "just the fact that I come to worship means that I have fellowship with God." I believe we look too much on the outside of our actions instead of on the inside to see what our hearts reveal as our true love. Many church folks profess faith without the possession of the Lord; therefore, there is something missing in their lives.

I came to this realization shortly after Mary and I were married and it made all the difference in my life. When I gave Christ my life, I allowed Him to completely take charge of my being; therefore, that void, that something missing, was found and with it my ultimate purpose as I faced a cruel world. It was then I dedicated myself to raising my children, if God allowed us the privilege, to know and to serve Him. I asked for God's guidance and wisdom when I became the leader of a household with children, as I firmly believe this is one of the most important responsibilities there is in life. I have not always made the right decisions. I was by far not perfect in my leadership role as a father, but I am so proud of each one of my boys. They have become leaders of respect and integrity who faithfully serve our Lord. They are men of God.

However, I must admit that even though I follow Christ as Lord, I, like Job, sometimes turn from God with impatience, pride, frustration, and a host of other things. I know many who read this also face that same challenge in life. I want to address that as we journey through the life of a hero who persevered through the very same things we face.

On April 14, 1974, we worshipped at the little Baptist church where I was pastor (we had just been called by the congregation) and the day was a beautiful Easter Sunday. I remember it was one of the most perfect spring days I had ever lived. We had a great day at church or, at least, I thought so since I was the pastor. We came home to our fifty-foot mobile home that night and collapsed on the bed. We were especially tired from having a sunrise service along with the regular morning and evening services. I know Mary was tired, she had reached the nine-month point in her first pregnancy, and looked as though she had the whole kitchen sink up front on her tummy. And then it happened about 11:00 p.m.; the dam burst. Her water broke and we were beginning a journey in life that will be with us until we get to heaven's door and even beyond, as Josh made it to heaven before we did.

The three greatest days of my life were when each of our three boys was born. I sometimes cannot remember what I did yesterday, but I can recapture every minute and detail of my sons' births. Back then, we dad's weren't allowed in the delivery room when our children were being born, so I couldn't see Josh until sometime later, after they had checked him out and cleaned him up.

I was standing outside the nursery on that Monday morning —April 15, 1974 — when our pediatrician, Dr. Sims, whom I had not met, came walking up with my son in his arms. He looked so at ease, very casual. I remember thinking he was a janitor, but why was he carrying that beautiful baby in his arms? Should he not be carrying a mop or something other than a baby? These people let just anybody take care of their babies. "Mr. Byers?" How did the janitor know my name and, again, what is he doing with that very handsome child? "I am Dr. Sims, and here is your beautiful baby boy. He is doing just great even though they had just a little bit of trouble getting him through the threshold as you can see by the marks on his face, but that is no problem, as the marks will soon go away." Boy was I shocked. I did not move for a few seconds, as I just was not expecting this "having a baby" deal to go down like this. He pushed Josh in my arms, as I stood there in total amazement of this creature ... this thing ... this tiny human being. I had never held a newborn baby before, and there he was, in full color, looking up at me like, "Well, here I am. What do you think?" Josh was born at 7:48 a.m., weighing in at seven pounds, twelve ounces, and was nineteen inches long.

There I stood at the hospital in Anderson, South Carolina with tear-filled eyes looking down at my first son. I stood with awestruck countenance realizing a miracle had just taken place. A miracle that could only happen because of our great and Almighty God. I was humbled as I stared into the eyes of Joshua Todd Byers, not yet knowing I stared into the eyes of a hero …

"The time of discipline began. Each of us the pupil of whichever one of us could best teach what each of us needed to learn."
-Maria Isabel Barreno

CHAPTER TWO

GROWING UP

"I pray that out of his glorious riches he may strengthen
you with power through his Spirit in your inner being."
Ephesians 3:16 NIV

When our boys were growing up, they all got caught up in the superhero shows, with good reason, since their father loved *Superman*®. I used to watch *Superman*® faithfully when I got home from school (it was in black and white, but I did not know the difference). I remember when the *Incredible Hulk*® came on television, we would all get in front of that television set as if it were a god and we were worshipping, much to the displeasure of Mom. None of the four of us could wait until the Hulk got mad, and then watch out!

We all are guilty of desperately wanting the good guy to win. Now, we love the fight and the battle scenes, but in the end, we want the guy with the white hat to come out on top. You know, that is how the movie people make so much money—our thirst for a fight with the good guy winning. I think maybe that is why we are so fascinated with super strength coming from superheroes. We idolize the power of this person, this thing, as they overcome evil in the world. We fantasize ourselves into being strong enough to solve the world's problems. It is so frustrating when we cannot even solve our own problems that we daydream about outrunning locomotives, jumping high buildings, and speeding faster than a bullet. The real battle we face is the battle inside, the evil of depression that tries constantly to defeat us and cause the erosion of faith as it begins to collapse under the pressures of a troubled soul.

The Apostle Paul talked about the Ephesians being strengthened in the inner man by God's Spirit. As we allow God to totally permeate our souls, we begin to conquer the demon inside our lives. The conquest of inner space deep down in our souls is the most significant thing that can happen to us. We can put as many men, women and pieces of hardware out into the great universe as we want, but that will not solve our real problems. The real problems rest in the inner space of our hearts. We need the strength and the power Paul talked about within us to face the demons of depression and the evils that are determined to destroy us.

As Mary and I drove up the driveway of the Alewine's home with baby Josh, Rev. and Mrs. Alewine (Mary's parents) lived in a parsonage owned by the church, (Mr. Alewine was also a minister) Mrs. "A" was anxiously waiting for us. She ran to the car door reaching her arms out for the precious baby. Her tears of joy flowed as she held her grandson; then Mary started to cry. Well, I cried too but for a much different reason. I had received Josh's dismissal papers when we left the hospital, and I was looking at the cost of having a baby. My parents would talk about having children at home and that might not be a bad idea. No, I have to admit I would have never survived the ordeal at home without doctors or nurses. Anyway, I thank God for health insurance!

Josh grew up as a healthy, perfect little boy. We lived in the parsonage where I was pastor and one could not ask for a better life. Our church was out in the country just a few miles from two towns; halfway between Greenwood and Abbeville, South Carolina. Our home was right beside the church on three acres and just a fantastic place to raise children. In fact, we were there for every one of our boys' births. Josh had a cocker spaniel named Hogan, and he would go outside in the back yard and play with Hogan for hours. Unfortunately, one day after about two years Hogan got out of the fenced-in area and ran out into the busy highway and was immediately run over by the passing traffic. He died instantly. Josh faced his very first crisis. I had to go pick Hogan up off the highway and dreaded telling Josh that he was gone to doggy Heaven. Josh had such a tender heart, and we had to console him it seemed forever. He cried and cried. The only solution was to go to The Humane Society and get another dog. That's when Pepper became a part of Josh's life. A hero saves one from destruction and this is the first of a series of heroic actions.

One day Josh walked in the kitchen where his mom was busily working and announced that he wanted a pig. It was out of the blue, and I am sure he got it on his mind when I read him his favorite book about farm animals. His mother tried to explain to him that we could not just go get a pig for the backyard, but Josh always needed an explanation and it usually wasn't good enough; so he continued to beg for a pig. Finally, in frustration he used his Daddy's pitch line he had heard hundreds of times when folks would leave church and share a need. I would always say to them that I would pray about that. Josh announced to his mom that since she would not get him a pig, "I'll just ask Jesus for the pig." Amazingly enough, Jesus would see to it that he got his pig. He prayed that night for a pig and quickly went sound to sleep with confidence and assurance that the pig would be there in the morning.

Mary came and shared with me Josh's prayer and said that we may have a dilemma on our hands in trying to explain to Josh why there wasn't going to be a pig. Early the next morning, which happened to be a Sunday morning, Mary was in the kitchen preparing breakfast when Josh came running in and immediately looked out the window to the backyard. He began to shout, "Mommy, Jesus done brought me a pig." Mary ran to see what was going on and sure enough there inside our backyard fence was a little pig. About that time, I walked back in the door from having gone out to the church to unlock the doors and get things ready for services that day. I thought something horrible had happened because the look on Mary's face was dreadful and confused. I ran to see what was going on and she just pointed out through the window into the backyard, and I saw the pig! We were both speechless but Josh was ecstatic and anxious to get outside to pet his pig. Once we got ourselves together we took him out, and all marveled at the beautiful pig that Jesus had brought to Josh overnight. We later found out that our neighbor who lived down a long dirt road in front of us had a hole in his fence that kept a sow (mother pig) and her babies. When the neighbor saw that the pig was at our house, he asked if it would be okay if he left it there until sometime the next day so he could repair his fence. That two days was all Josh needed because his innocent childlike prayer had been answered and he was content. A hero has a faith that is most unbelievable...

When Josh was about four years old, it was wintertime and we had a gigantic ice storm. It began as freezing rain, then snow, followed by three inches of sleet and ice. I remember it was Thursday and I needed to walk to my study at the church and begin preparing for the coming Sunday sermon. As I was getting dressed, Josh asked where I was going and when he found out that I was going out to the church, he started begging to get out in the snow and ice. I learned early on with my children if there is an opportunity to spend time with them, I did. I do not regret that now for sure. His mother began the process of putting enough clothes on him to stay warm and we started on our little journey, Josh looking like a spaceman walking on the moon. As we got out in the elements of an icy cold wind and navigating the slippery terrain, Josh began to pull away from me as I held his hand. "Daddy, I want to walk by myself. Let me go… Let me go." I tried to explain that he would fall and get hurt unless I had him in my grip. He finally pulled himself free from my hand and took off. It did not take but a few seconds, and he was on his rear, crying like the world had just come to an end. I immediately knelt down, picked him up and stroked his *owie*. I didn't scold him or say I told you so, even though it ran through my mind. When he finally stopped crying, as we were sitting on the ice in that cold wind, he looked at me eyeball-to-eyeball and said, "Daddy, from now on, would you hold on to me?"

I guess one of the most frustrating hurts I have as I grieve his loss today is that I could not hold him there in Iraq. I couldn't make sure he was okay. I couldn't be there when my hero, my boy got his final *owie*…

Around the age of five, Josh began saying that he wanted to be a soldier and serve his country. His patriotism was strong even as a young boy, and he continually talked about loving his country and wanting to be a soldier when he grew up. As time went on and we continued to hear these statements from our oldest son, we told ourselves that it was the passing fantasy of a young boy. He played with *G.I. Joe*® toys and loved to watch the *Star Wars*® movies and anything about soldiers and war. This love of country and desire to serve his country only grew stronger as he got older, and we began asking ourselves, "What if he does this?" The total acceptance on our part to see and understand what Josh was called to do would be years later with an ache in our hearts as we told him we would support him in whatever decision he made about serving in the military.

When Josh was nine years old, the Lord opened the door for us to move to Georgetown, South Carolina. This was a really old town, named after King George of England, and was located on the coast. Josh excelled in school and sports. He began to understand the concept of reaching for excellence in life, something that took me at least to the age of 21. He was very motivated in everything he did and took even the smallest things to heart. The last baseball game he played in the season of his fifth-grade year was proof of his emotions about something he loved so much. He missed a pop-up in the outfield that caused the opponent to win. When we met him after the coach dismissed the team, he turned on the waterworks in tears as he took it so personally. That is what heroes do...

He loved baseball. As I talked to his fellow soldiers after his death, one thing that was always mentioned by most of them was his love of baseball. One day I saw him (he was still in elementary school) writing a letter, and I inquired about to whom he was writing. He replied that he was asking Hank Aaron, probably the greatest player to play the game of baseball, for his autograph. I laughed and said Hank would never see the letter. It took several months, but guess whose autograph we received in the mail? We now have it sitting in our bedroom as a reminder that heroes have a determination that will always win...

"It matters not how strait the gate, How charged with punishments the scroll, I am the master of my fate; I am the captain of my soul."
-W.E. Henley

CHAPTER THREE

IT WAS AN UNUSUAL EARLY DECISION, BUT FINAL

"Blessed are those who hunger and thirst for
righteousness, for they will be filled." Matthew 5:6 NIV

The righteousness Jesus talks about here in the Sermon on the Mount is a desire to be finally free from damning sin, because sin separates us from God (the sin that keeps us from belonging to God). It is desiring to be what God intends us to be. In the original text of the Greek language, the word used here means to hunger after the whole loaf of bread or to thirst after the entire glass of water. It's meaning is to not be content with a piece of bread or a taste of water. The whole of this Scripture is a spirit of conquest. It is a fact that happiness is not something we should seek out directly. Happiness is always something that results from seeking something else, even though that something is not pleasant at the time. We notice in the Scripture that Jesus did not say to seek after happiness, money, or popularity, but He emphasized righteousness. Also note that it is not happiness that comes to one who has righteousness but to one who hungers and thirsts for it. Jesus continues by saying they are the ones who will be satisfied. Jesus was saying the more one is filled, the more one is satisfied, and the more one is hungering and thirsting. We know that the average, intelligent agnostic would say this is way too much of a paradox to be true; yet, I have seen this happen time and time again in my ministry.

It was beautiful as I was driving home after a long day of visiting hospitals and nursing homes checking on those who were sick and lonely.

I have to admit many times I would go in the room to be a blessing and come away being blessed by those who were persevering in the midst of pain and suffering. I decided that if my wife had not prepared a meal that I would surprise the whole gang with a, "Hey, let's go out to eat!" In the early '80s that was a real treat at our house. Kids today just yawn and say, "Okay, if you want to." Mary had not cooked simply because she did not know what time I would be home. When I made my announcement, the boys excitedly shouted, "yeah" and Mary shouted silently within her heart. We all piled in my *Chevy Chevette*® (I always wanted a 'vette) and drove toward the town and the restaurants. As we approached the main intersection where we had to make a decision, I simply asked, "Where do you want to go?" I guess that was one of the dumbest questions I have ever asked a bunch of boys who only think on the fast food mode and a young mother, dainty lady who thinks only on the spinach salad mode. The closer I got to the main intersection, the more I had boys shouting in my ear, "I want to go to *Pizza Hut*®. No, not me I want *McDonalds*®. "No, no, I want to go to *Burger King*®." "Now, boys be quiet. Honey, I want to go to *Ryan's*® to get that fresh salad." The closer we got to the main intersection the louder I heard everyone's plea. I got totally confused, perplexed and just plain beside myself and made a wrong turn at the intersection (wrong way on a one-way street). Frustrated we went home, where we ate peanut butter and jelly sandwiches. I learned a valuable lesson that day. You should always decide where you are going before you ever leave the house!

This is such an important principle in our daily lives as we face unknown demons hurling themselves at us at every turn. Just as children screaming in our ears and a dear, sweet lady quietly insisting on some place else, we are left with indecision, and not knowing where to turn. We approach a main intersection in life, and we make the wrong turn. When we turn in the wrong direction, many times we are left with nothing but sandwiches instead of a "meat and three." It is very important to decide what we are going to do, where we are going, which way we need to turn at the main intersection of life, before we make a huge mistake. We need to always remind ourselves of where we are going. That is what heroes do…

In the summer of 1986 we felt the calling of God to move from the coast of South Carolina to the upstate of South Carolina to a place called Spartanburg, a town about 200 miles away. We accepted the call to come as pastor of the West Main Baptist Church in downtown Spartanburg. Mary and I were excited because for the first time in our ministry this was a church that didn't have a parsonage for us to live in, but they gave us a housing allowance to buy our own home. Living in a church-owned home can sometimes be like living in a fish bowl. Everyone watches the pastor's family and tries to catch them being human. Our boys were very excited about living in a new area and making new friends.

We found a comfortable home in a little town called Wellford. It was about eight miles from our church and had about an acre of land that backed up to a creek and thick woods. It was a friendly and nice, quiet neighborhood. Our garage was separate from the house and the boys had a great play area in the front and back yards.

Josh began the seventh grade at D. R. Hill Middle School, about five miles from where we lived. He was a little apprehensive about the first day of school, but that quickly gave way to confidence and excitement about his new future. He loved his school and his grades reflected an ambitious, young, rising star among his peers. He made lifelong relationships there.

During this time of days being filled with good friends and enjoying a nice home without the fish bowl stigma, all of our boys flourished in Wellford. Josh and Milam played baseball in their respective age groups in the spring and football in the fall. We stayed busy with school, friends, and sports year round. During the summer we would go to our favorite rental condo in Garden City Beach, South Carolina and enjoy our vacation time together.

It is important to note that while we all loved our home life, it was a different story entirely in our life at the church, and that was tough since that was my job. Our church members in general were rather distant and did not really want to grow or add new people to the membership. Most of them were content to just drift along like a piece of driftwood tumbling on to the seashore pushed along by the rolling tide. They were always formal and professional, insisting on calling me "Dr. Byers" and never opened up to our family with loving acceptance and our boys readily picked up on this. Therefore, all of our boys, even Spanky (aka Jared), our 4-year-old, began disliking going to church. If a young person did something naughty, one of our boys was quickly blamed for it no matter who did it. We worked out a little game to help them deal with "immature adults" by letting each of them choose where we would go out to eat lunch after church on Sundays. Josh always loved the local diner with its "meat and three," Milam loved the steak-house buffet, and Jared chose the pizza place. It may sound trite to do but it worked and gave them all something to look forward to each Sunday.

One day in the fall of 1986, Josh came home all excited about an air show demonstration that was going to take place at Shaw Air Force Base in Sumter, South Carolina, about two hours from where we lived. He and his best friend Cale (still a close family friend) wanted to attend. They were both seventh graders and like most young guys they thought jets, fighting, and soldiers were very exciting. Cale's family took them to the air show and Josh came home with a determined look about him (I learned later to accept it) that I noticed but shrugged off at the time as just a young person's fantasy. He told his mom and me that he had decided what he wanted to do for a career; he wanted to serve his country in the military.

We were constantly being shown folders and information that Josh had picked up at school or had written to the military academies for. He already knew that he wanted to be a pilot and attend the best school in the world for pilots – The United States Air Force Academy in Colorado Springs, Colorado. He was so absorbed in committing to the military for life that it was all he talked about and dreamed about. He would go to sleep every night reading encyclopedias and very often he looked at the information in them about all of the service academies. He found out what the requirements were for getting into an academy, and he was determined to go for it. He never changed his mind or wavered from that goal he had set for himself in the seventh grade. He wanted to serve his country and later, to give his life for his country to protect our freedom in a hate-filled world.

Josh decided early on where he was going to turn at the main intersection of life. He knew his destiny and where he was going.

That is what heroes do...

"It is not enough to take steps which may someday lead to a goal; each step must be itself a goal and a step likewise."
-Goethe

CHAPTER FOUR

YOU ARE ACCEPTED AND APPOINTED

"Now Jericho was tightly shut up because of the
Israelites. No one went out and no one came in."
Joshua 6:1 NIV

At this point in the Old Testament of God's Word in the Book of Joshua,
Joshua had received his orders, after the Israelites had wandered in the
desert for forty years, to go forward and begin to take the Promised Land
called Canaan. After crossing the Jordan River, they came upon their first
obstacle. It's name was Jericho; a walled city. And a fortified city it was,
ready to take the strongest of armies as they were locked behind these
massive walls. The Israelites checked them out. These walls were so massive
they could not tunnel under them as they were too deep, they could not
climb the walls as they were so steep, and they could not dig through
them. What was Joshua to do? The children of God could not inherit the
Promised Land if they did not deal with Jericho. How would these massive
walls be dealt with barring a miracle? Jericho became the place for them to
either go on with God in the face of war, fighting huge obstacles but with
faith in God who could literally make the walls fall down or learn to be
content wandering in the wilderness with no real purpose or direction.

We all arrive there at some point, don't we? There comes a time for
all of us at some particular place or situation that demands of us to go
on...or...turn back and wander in the wilderness with no real purpose
or direction in our lives. Heroes keep moving forward, they go on... and

thank God they did, as God had a plan to knock down the walls so the Israelites could walk over the fallen walls and capture the enemy. The city was captured and the army was successful because they trusted their God. That is what heroes do....

One of the most memorable times in our life is the move we made from Spartanburg, South Carolina, all the way to Reno-Sparks, Nevada. It was a challenging career move for me as we entered the mission field that was so ripe for harvest. I had really felt the Lord calling us to be a part of the church planting movement several years prior. After many years of praying, when this position opened for a church planter in Nevada we got the green light from God to go. We did have to throw in a little faith. We sold the very first house we had ever owned, and moved to a city out west with a new culture that we had absolutely no clue about dealing with the now (or then) generation.

Josh was really excited about making the move. As we traveled toward Reno, he was always joking and in my opinion, Josh was one of the best impressionists I have ever known. He could talk like just about anybody, especially my pastor friends (that was funny only if "you had been there"). We moved to a rental house on Sells Street in Sparks, Nevada and began making a home there. We got all the boys signed up in school and found out that we needed to get up to date on their shots at the health department. Josh thought he was covered and began to rag Milam and Jared about how much it would hurt. As the lady was going over their records, she looked at Josh and said, "You will need a shot in a few months, so we might as well go ahead and get it done." I thought I would fall over laughing as the shoe was on the other foot. I wish you could have seen the expression on his face.

What happened after their first day of school will haunt me for the rest of my life. My boys were treated like they had some sort of disease. In fact, the main teasing was for their Southern accent. We were all born someplace and have absolutely nothing to do with who or where we were born. But yet, some people with their noses sticking high in the air begin to judge who we are. We still have a lot of prejudice problems in our nation and I can understand why. I personally do not think we will ever get over that conflict among our own American people. We heard from all three of our boys about how unwelcoming the guys and gals were to them. It was especially tough though for Josh; he was caught off guard kind of like being blindsided. It wasn't D.R. Hill or Byrnes High School in South Carolina and his friends were many miles away. He just hadn't expected the traumatic changes that were occurring in his life. He was feeling so all alone.

Reed High School in Sparks, Nevada was located in a new section of the city and it was an upper middle class neighborhood. We were barely into the zoned area for Reed High School, which thanks to advice from a friend, put our kids in a much better and safer school environment. We met Josh for lunch on his first day. Reed had "open lunch" meaning the students could leave campus during lunchtime and there were a bunch of fast food restaurants just across the street. Milam and Jared were younger and we knew they would be okay after a few days, but Mary and I both had this eerie uneasiness about Josh. We met him at the local sub-sandwich shop and (talk about an awkward uneasiness as we sat) I began the slide down when I asked how was it going. He looked at me, then his mom and his eyes filled up. All of a sudden he burst out sobbing and sobbing. Josh was tenderhearted but he very seldom cried; in fact, he had never wept in this manner. Mary and I knew this was not normal but had no idea what we would face during the next several months.

As the days slowly passed, Josh's regular routine began when school was over, he would not talk. He would not talk or play around with his brothers at home. He had dropped headfirst into a deep depression and the scary thing was he was still falling and we did not know what to do. He would not play sports, he did not watch television, and made absolutely no effort to reach out and try to find a friend. He joined Naval Junior Reserve Officers Training Corps (NJROTC) when he got his schedule the first day, but after a few days; he dropped it. The most worrisome time of the day for us was not while he was in school but when he went to bed at night. He would lie there and moan, cry, and moan some more. The *walls* around him were well fortified and we needed a miracle to knock down the obstacle that headed him into a dangerous depression. Mary and I prayed, we hurt, we cried alone and with him. He was not himself and frankly did not care about anything anymore. It had been several weeks and he was progressively getting worse. All of a sudden, it happened, like walking into a huge hornet's nest that you just did not see coming. Mary and I took turns getting up at all hours of the night checking on him, for days to weeks to months. We would pat his back, cry with him, console him, promised to get him things he at one time or another had wanted. None of that mattered to him anymore. One night Mary went in to check on him and he told her that life just was not worth living anymore. She saw a pocketknife clutched in his hand. We had dreaded and prayed he would not hit that bottom. Josh had gotten lower that night than he had ever experienced. That is what heroes experience…

God comes through and answers our prayers on His time schedule and how it is best for our particular situation, not necessarily like we want Him to. We have this idea that we really know what is best for us and this is what needs to happen to solve our problems when only God knows everything and most of all He can see tomorrow and believe me, HE KNOWS WHAT IS BEST FOR HIS CHILDREN. Our part is to trust and I know that is not easy, but He is there for us and we have to walk by faith trusting Him to hold our hand and guide us. God's plan is always best. Maybe it doesn't seem so to us at the time, but He loves us more than we can ever imagine with our finite minds; therefore, we wait, persevere, and wait some more until God is ready to move.

With heavy hearts about "What are we going to do?" going through our minds, work did not matter any more, I wanted my family well and happy because they came first. I have always lived with my top three priorities in life: my personal walk with God, my family, then my job. I sat down with Josh and completely opened my heart. I had already prayed and talked with Mary about what I had decided to do, and it was simply that we needed to leave Nevada and go back home to South Carolina. As soon as I shared that bit of news, Josh looked as though I had hit him in the head with a 2 x 4 board. He was stunned, then his countenance changed and he began to smile. "I am going home." As if to say, "I get to go back to the wilderness that I know so well and be comfortable with no real direction for the future, but I will be in familiar surroundings."

The next day I went to a missionary meeting about strategy planning in reaching the 50,000 people who were right in the middle of an area where there was not one evangelical church except for the one I was commissioned to start. During the break I met a Christian psychologist who had recently moved from Los Angeles. We seemed to hit it off, and he became a very good friend. God was lining up His soldiers to march around the walls because they were going to come down, only on His terms. One day we were having lunch, and this new friend offered the waiting room of his office for us to use for our very first place of worship without cost. I began to share with him that it sounded exciting, but that I was having some family problems and would be leaving. He had this way, I guess you might call it training, to get me to open up and unload. I did unload and unload. I know physically I wasn't lighter but mentally and emotionally I felt I had lost 50 pounds of weight off my shoulders. He said, "Let me talk to Josh and I want this to be a professional discount (no charge); so you will not have to worry about your budget." What a blessing this man was, an angel God used to knock down those walls in Josh's life. Josh reached out for help and that's what heroes do…

I found out later that Josh had made up his mind to make the best of school even though he was depressed, but he was so concerned about me leaving a ministry God had called us to that was truly a Godly thing. When God brought the psychologist into the mix, that was the answer to move Josh's slump out of the ditch so he could start moving forward. God wants us to make those decisions, make those moves and He will get us through. I am amazed at the many people over the years I have encountered in my ministry that just sit back with the attitude, "OK, God if you want to do something, then go ahead You do it. I will just sit here and wait." It just doesn't work that way. We have to jump in over our heads and allow God to hold our hands as we travel in the depths of life's journey. That is what heroes do…they move forward.

After going through the move and dealing with "acceptance" in a new place, the boys found friends and began loving the West. Josh still didn't have a close friend that he could trust and confide in since we had moved to Nevada. He really longed for someone to go to lunch with during school, to just hang out with whenever. Josh was at his desk one day after seven months in school and glanced over at a guy's desk beside him and noticed a sticker of a Christian rock group on his notebook. When class was over, Josh immediately introduced himself to Beau Elsfelder, who became Josh's best friend in high school. Beau is 6 feet 10 inches tall and a truly delightful young man. He too was looking for a real friend and he was raised in Reno. Josh invited Beau to church the next Sunday, Beau soon made a commitment to Christ as he had not been to church much growing up. It wasn't long before Beau's brother, Noah, and his parents became faithful to church. Josh was always trying to get young people to church. He was determined to help us build something we had started from scratch…that's what heroes do…

The next school year, Josh was improving and was more comfortable with his surroundings and signed up for NJROTC. I remember he came home, excited with that all knowing grin, to show off his uniform. His teacher, Commander Jobe, was such a great help to Josh and guided him toward his future military career. Josh soon jumped through the ranks as he soaked up anything and everything military.

Josh's teacher for NJROTC was Commander Gordon Jobe, who was such a blessing and tremendous support for him during those years of high school. During Josh's memorial service in Reno after his funeral in South Carolina, Commander Jobe shared this eulogy about Josh:

My first meeting with Josh Byers occurred a little over fourteen years ago at the start of the spring semester of school year 1989-1990 at Reed High School. His courtesy and friendly demeanor immediately impressed me. Obviously, this quality young man would be a definite asset to the NJROTC program of which I was the head instructor. So I was greatly disappointed when he came in a little while later, I don't recall if it was a matter of a few days or a couple of weeks, and stated that he was going to transfer to another class for personal reasons. He said that he would return and re-enroll in the fall. My thoughts were probably along the lines of "yeah, right! How many times have I heard that one?" However, I probably said something like, "You have to decide for yourself what is best for you to do with your life."

At the start of the fall semester, I got my first lesson of the quality of Josh Byers' character. He re-enrolled just as he said he would. Josh obviously was not one to make commitments lightly and could be depended upon to carry them out. He became very actively involved in the Unit, joining the drill team which he commanded in his junior year, participating in many community service activities, field trips, parades, and just about anything else that we did. He maintained this level of activity throughout his entire time at Reed. I suspected that his "personal reasons' might have been a little culture shock of having moved from South Carolina to the high desert west halfway through a school year.

As he progressed through his high school years at Reed, he also became very active in other activities such as the Honor Society, Physics Club, Young Republicans, and Peer Assistants, while maintaining

an excellent academic record. He became very well known at the school and developed an outstanding reputation of integrity, courtesy, cooperation, and charity. One of his classmates remarked to me recently, "I remember Josh as being a wonderful friend who was always nice and charismatic -- someone that you would be proud to call a friend." Another comment from a teacher: "I just remember how nice and polite he was. Always ready to do something for someone."

Josh developed such an outstanding reputation that in his senior year he was elected to the office of Student Body President and was selected at the same time to be the cadet commander of the NJROTC Unit. This was the first (and last) time that anyone had held both of those offices simultaneously.

As confident as he was in his outstanding qualities, Josh also showed humility. He demonstrated this to me at the end of his junior year. In order to give me some insight as to how the leadership of the unit for the following year would shape up, I had developed a peer group rating of several leadership qualities. I listed the present junior class alphabetically and instructed them to reorder the list as to how they felt their peers rated in the qualities listed. One of the qualities was loyalty. A classmate of Josh's was a mild Downs Syndrome challenged person who demonstrated exceptional loyalty to the unit. Josh came to me after the rating and said that he had rated that person the highest in that quality even ahead of himself because no one is more loyal than that person.

I too was the beneficiary of his generosity. Normally, graduates who have excelled in one or more areas receive various awards, scholarships, and other recognitions. Just prior to his graduation, Josh presented me with a poster with the inscription, "The greatest influence on my desire to become a military officer." This shall remain one of my most cherished possessions.

At the memorial service at Fort Carson, Colorado, on July 30, there were many mentions of Josh's qualities. A fellow officer stated that Josh was "one of the best and brightest…" However, I found in the 1992 Reed High School yearbook this statement that I think sums up best all of the accolades:

Dear Josh,
You've always done your best: an appointment to West Point is the result. We are proud of you because you did it with character and integrity. Always remember we love you and that "I can do all things through Christ…"
Love,
Mom, Dad, Milam & Jared

The untimely loss of such a fine and wonderful person saddens us all deeply. However, I believe that although he is no longer physically present among us he will be always with us through his influence on our lives. I know that he profoundly influenced me and I will be grateful for the rest of my life for the privilege of playing a small role in his life.
Gordon A. Jobe
Lt. Cmdr., U.S. Navy (retired)

Reed High School was a huge school to us and I think in most districts as well. Reed had around 2,200 students and it was easy to go unnoticed. Josh was determined to follow to the nth degree the rules to getting in one of four military academies, which states that the applicant must be active in sports, student government, and a host of things offered in school. They look for the best all around student, not just an egghead. Josh excelled in his grades, NJROTC, sports (he loved baseball as I have stated), and many extracurricular activities. He was active in church and did a number of things outside of school. It is very difficult to get accepted into an academy, but I figured all the things Josh was involved with were sufficient. But it wasn't for Josh. That's how heroes think…

Josh came home from school one day in his junior year with that determined look that I was beginning to see often. He announced to his mom and me that he had decided to run for school president, serving during his senior year. I really regret what I did next, I laughed with a sensible explanation that most of the students (2,200 of them) did not know him. He was an outsider even though we had lived there over two years and would have to win over the majority of students to vote for him. Mary and I both tried to get him to run for secretary, treasurer or vice-president -- not the most difficult office there is. We also discovered that if there was a dominant religious group in western Nevada (95% were unchurched) it would be the Mormon church and Brigham Young University would automatically present a full-ride scholarship to a Mormon who is elected president at Reed High School as Reed was an academically acclaimed public high school. In other words, as the all-knowing example of a father I was demonstrating, I declared that would be an impossible task to accomplish. Josh grinned with a determined steady look on his face and replied that it was not impossible. He proceeded to take his own money he had saved up and made posters to put all over the school, I mean professional looking posters with pictures and witty promises. I was astonished at the hard work this took and especially the determination I witnessed. His main opponent was a young man who was a Mormon and his parents got involved (Duh...wonder why) with a lot of expense going to posters and candy handed out to those promising their vote. He outspent Josh two to one in campaign expenses and yes, this is a high school election. Election day finally arrived and the results were amazing. Out of about four or five students running, the outcome came down to a runoff between this young man and Josh. Again, we went through tons of pressure in the Byers' household until the next election. When the day rolled around, Josh had to leave to attend a conference for officers on student council in California. One of the vice-principals called to give us the results. Josh had won President of the Reed Student Body for 1991-1992. He went on to tell us that Josh was his pick and the one who deserved to win and he said, "Good always wins." I immediately asked Josh if he would forgive me for not believing, and I would never make that mistake again even if he announced he wanted to be President of the United States. I was truly taken aback at a young man's determination... That is what heroes have...

As Josh labored through his high school years, his accomplishments were quite amazing. He was asked to serve as the student representative on the board for the entire Washoe County School System, which included nine high schools at the time, after which he underwent an extensive selection process where he competed among the top students in the district. The interesting thing about Josh, which was unusual compared to most teenagers, was the fact that he loved to be interviewed. It seemed like he thrived on the interaction of being questioned, and he loved to share his opinion about subjects that he knew about, which he did not take lightly because of his study and research. We had to go out and buy him a suit and he sat beside the school district's attorney during school board meetings. The elected school board always checked with Josh about his thoughts and his opinion held a lot of weight. It seemed there was a lot of controversy during Josh's senior year, for which he shared a caring student's wisdom concerning the subject. Josh also served as the Commander of the NJROTC unit at Reed. Commander Jobe was thrilled over Josh's accomplishments as no other NJROTC student had ever been student body president and commander of the unit. Josh also served as commander on the NJROTC drill team which won quite a few awards that year.

During the fall of Josh's senior year came the biggest news in his life up to that time. He had applied to two of the service academies, knowing the Air Force would not be interested in him as a pilot since he was nearsighted in his vision. He had taken all the physicals, finished the application process, which was a difficult feat in itself, and finished his interviews with our two Senators and Congresswoman. He did an incredible job in preparing and working toward the goal he had since the seventh grade. That is what heroes do...

Josh was nominated by Nevada's two U.S. Senators, one Congresswoman, and also received a nomination from the Secretary of the Navy. The United States Military Academy at West Point was the first to send an acceptance letter with the Naval Academy at Annapolis acceptance coming a few weeks later. It is an unbelievable accomplishment since over 20,000 apply to each academy and only 1,200 are selected for each one. When Josh learned he would not be able to be a pilot at the beginning of his freshmen year in high school, he wanted to attend the Naval Academy since he was in NJROTC at Reed High School. He was sent to Newport, Rhode Island, the summer before being a senior to participate in a mini Officers Candidate School (OCS) for which only a very few were selected all over the U.S. to compete (he was one of two that were selected out of ten western states). After he graduated from intense Naval training, he began to question the prospect of being at sea 6-8 months out of the year. He also did not like the changes that had been made to the honor code at the Naval Academy as West Point's was much more strict. Josh was big on duty, honor, and country. That is what heroes are made of…

We face walls through all of life that stop us, and it is impossible to progress and move forward unless we have the faith to knock them down; otherwise, we wander in the desert with no real direction or purpose. By faith in God, the walls come tumbling down and they still fall today if we exercise the faith. We keep moving forward with a determined faith and spirit. That is what heroes do…

"Expect great things from God and attempt great things for God, because that brings honor to the Lord"
-William Carey

CHAPTER FIVE

WEST POINT: DUTY, HONOR, COUNTRY

"According to your faith, let it be done to you."
Matthew 9:29 NIV

I recently read an editorial that was written in the AAA magazine, *"Going Places,"* the November/December 2010 issue by John Tomlin, President and CEO, AAA Club South. (Mr. Tomlin shared with me, "I would be honored to have any part of my article used in "Keep Moving Forward".)

> ***The character of a Leader*** *-- I recently had the pleasure of touring the West Point Academy with my good friend Rolfe Arnhym, who was a cadet there in 1953. I've known Rolfe for many years and am always impressed with the pride he exudes when he talks about West Point. I have visited many fine universities with my three children, but something about this one was different. Yes, they are ranked as a top 10 school and offer a beautiful campus on the banks of the Hudson River. But many schools are highly ranked and surrounded by beauty. During our tour, some of the differences began to become clear.*
>
> *First, unlike other colleges, a physical fitness requirement assures the cadets can handle the physical and mental demands that will be placed on them at West Point and, later, as military leaders. However, what gave me the most pause was their focus on leadership. Their curriculum, honor*

> *code, activities and daily ritual are all designed to foster leadership and teamwork. The core mission of West Point is to develop leaders of character for our army - someone who knows what is right and possesses the moral courage to act on that knowledge. The principles of truthfulness, fairness, respect for others, and a personal commitment to maintaining these values constitute that fundamental ideal known as the Spirit of the Code... This excerpt from the Cadet Prayer is particularly meaningful to me and seems fitting during election season:*
>
> *"Make us choose the harder right instead of the easier wrong and never to be content with a half truth when the whole truth can be won."*

Faith is expecting the best, which increases your ability. The athlete who is famous for his/her play in whatever sport knows that the winning edge is attitude, not ability. You ask any coach worth his or her salt and they will quickly agree that attitude wins games. Mohammed Ali only lost two fights in his lifetime. Both of those fights had only one difference from all the other fights. In a press conference prior to the fight, he said, "Now, if I lose this fight..." This was the only time he ever said "if," and he lost them both. Faith is the key that unlocks all that God wants to do in your life.

One of the most popular stories in the Bible that just about everybody knows is David and Goliath. David was just a teenager when he arrived at the battlefield to do a chore his father sent him to do. He was astounded to learn that nobody would face the giant Goliath. David proceeded to find five smooth stones that would fit nicely in his slingshot and walked toward this man who stood nine feet tall. Note that he picked up five stones, not because he thought he might miss but Goliath had four brothers. David's attitude was that he would just take out the whole family. His attitude was remarkable. David looked at this problem, not troubled that he would lose, but confident that God was on his side! It blesses and encourages my heart to read this Scripture again and again because David showed the right attitude, the winning spirit to accomplish the seemingly impossible task before him. That is what heroes do...

It was June 26, 1992, a Friday when we arrived at JFK airport in New York City to take Josh to West Point. We would soon learn that WestPoint was not a "normal" college as Josh began to undergo the rigorous life required of a New Cadet. We made sure that the whole family would go as we prepared to say goodbye to our oldest son and Milam and Jared's oldest brother. We seemed to proceed through the trip with our scale of emotions at full blast. We wanted to arrive a few days early before "R" (reception) day so we could be together as a family. As I drove the rental car through this huge city, there were very few words spoken. We enjoyed the sights and did what we had planned. We spent two nights in Hackensack, New Jersey, before making the journey to West Point. We stayed at The Thayer Hotel, a historic inn on the grounds of West Point brimming with history. We arrived on Sunday afternoon and checked in. In the lobby, Josh encountered other soon-to-be cadets with the same emotions, and that night he met Abe Usher who became his best friend at West Point. I believe God lined them up to meet, they were alike in many ways. We also met Abe's parents and brother who were experiencing similar emotions as ours. What a blessing it was for us, especially Josh, to meet such an outstanding Christian family.

Early the next morning, June 29 was THE day. The procedure was to meet at the gymnasium for Josh to check in, find his company, and say goodbye to loved ones. As I write, I'm reminded of this being one of the toughest days in my life. Even when we said goodbye prior to him leaving for Iraq, we knew he was taken care of and of course, older with a wife. This time, he was still our son; the homebody. Josh loved to stay home on most weekends during his senior year just to be with us and watch a rented movie with his brothers and parents. Mary and I were facing the beginning of our empty-nest syndrome as Josh would be about 3,000 miles from us and could only come home at Christmas. I guess saying goodbye is one of the hardest experiences to deal with as a parent unless it is their child's funeral. I know it was the hardest thing he had faced up to this point in his life. But it was time to face this obstacle with faith. That is what heroes do...

We were standing in line at the gym, slowly winding our way inside, talking very little as we marched forward seemingly toward execution. Josh never lost his humor even in the most difficult of situations. Several of the friends with him during the last few hours he lived, shared some humorous times that had everyone laughing. As we slowly made our way inside, the academy had a small Army band playing. When we got closer and could hear the music wafting through the air, Josh chuckled and said, "Isn't that ironic?" I asked him what in the world he meant. He went on to explain that when the Titanic was going down in the ocean, a true tragedy, they had a small band playing attempting to calm the passengers.

Josh shared that it wasn't working for him. Neither was it working for us as we approached that dreaded moment. We cried and hugged saying our goodbyes and Josh disappeared up the bleachers marking the end of a tremendous period in our lives - he had left home. It was never the same. One could tell these young men and women displayed courage as they said their goodbyes. That is what heroes do...

Josh later told us that when they got upstairs behind the bleachers and the door closed, the upper classmen were waiting on them and the yelling started. The first-year cadet at West Point is called a plebe and they enter into summer training called "Beast Barracks." It was horrendous, demanding all one had to just hang in there. Some did not make it. The upper classmen ran the "show," they called the shots. Josh said later, much later, he fully understood why they did what they did, but not at the time he was going through it. They were building men and women to protect our country, not wimps — and that is not easy. On Sundays they were given a couple of hours to attend the church of their choice. Just about every cadet went to get away from the terror. And when they sat down in church after singing a few hymns, most started nodding from weariness. Josh called it an eyelid inspection. I cannot describe all that took place, but there are several great books out that detail the life of a cadet through their four years at West Point. I was amazed to hear what the plebes had to endure for the purpose of building a first-class soldier. That is what heroes do...

We were filled with anxiety while Josh was gone. We looked forward to his five-minute phone calls. There were times he did not think he could make it. We wrote him daily, sent encouraging cards, and asked his friends at church to continue writing him. As he got close to the end of "beast," he told us that he had decided to quit. This training had gotten the best of him, and he was homesick. He felt like it was time to come home and work toward another career. He claimed he might even become a pastor, oh, God forbid! In order for a new cadet to resign, he had to put on his dress uniform, shine his shoes, and ask for permission to speak to his superior. Josh said he got dressed up, shined his shoes spotless and asked permission to speak. Before Josh had a chance to unload, his commander (the upper classman), began to share in a decent and respectful manner that out of all the new cadets that he had dealt with — Josh was the best. He continued telling Josh that he had what it took to be a great officer and would make a difference in keeping our nation safe. The young upper classman stated emphatically that Josh had what it took to be the best leader he had trained; therefore, he gave him a great report, which was the envy of all new cadets.

Then he asked Josh what he wanted with him. Immediately Josh was reminded in his heart of why he was there and the special calling he had, including all of the dreams and commitments he had made. Josh replied, "Sir, I just wanted to know if I could do anything for you? Thank you, Sir, for your confidence in me. That's all, Sir." That was the turning point for Josh. He had believed all the upper classmen when they called the plebes weaklings and wimps and told them that they did not have what it takes and should quit because our country would be a lot better off. I guess they were tearing them down so they could build them back as real leaders. That's what heroes do…and Josh kept moving forward.

His four years at West Point were memorable to say the least. I was so proud of him. I became, and remain, the doting father. I would bring up the subject in any conversation. I know my church members were tired of hearing me talk about the experiences, but they were very supportive. They made it possible for Mary and me to visit Josh several times. When Josh would come home, they would all gather at the airport with banners and signs welcoming him back home to Nevada. It took so much courage for Josh to hang in there day after day, month after month, and year after year saying those difficult goodbyes. He would look back each time as he boarded the plane with a forlorn but determined expression. He exercised a tremendous faith walking out in the dark where he could not see. That is what heroes do…and Josh kept moving forward.

The students at West Point became family to each other. There was an active group of seven guys in the "Baptist Student Union (BSU);" a church denominational organization who were all in the class of '96'. They referred to themselves as the "Lucky Seven." They were like brothers during the bad times and good at "the Point."

One of the "Lucky Seven," Stan Hardee (from Cajun country in Louisiana), shared with us this story. "I remember when Josh had a date to a formal with a girl from Ole Miss, either yearling winter weekend or 500th night." (Note: "yearling" is a sophomore and "cow" is a junior at West Point which would be 500 days before graduation). "He was so pumped up about this girl who was supposedly a model. Josh told all the "Lucky Seven" and other cadets in BSU that he even had a picture of her in a sailor's outfit with a naughty smile. She looked gorgeous in the picture. It just so happened that I had to walk the area for some demerits I had received, so I was not allowed to go to the formal. However, I was determined to see this 'model', women are a rare treasure at West Point, especially Southern Belles. I asked Josh as a special favor if he would walk by the area while I was walking with my rifle on area tours, so I could see this gorgeous Ole Miss Southern Belle. I remember the day he brought her by … I could tell from far off that the picture she sent was not accurate, to say the least. I started laughing and thinking: 'I guess I am not the only one who is having a less than favorable weekend.' I could not wait until Sunday to hear Josh's version of what happened. He said, 'it was a nightmare,' when they went to the football game, 'she pulled out a can of snuff and stuffed a big wad of tobacco behind her lip then asked Josh if he wanted a dip.' Needless to say, this takes me back to those good times at 'the Point'!"

Every cadet has the opportunity to have a mentor, or as they call a sponsor, to be there when they need them. It was a home away from home, they could visit them on their times off and were welcomed as family. Josh had loving sponsors who meant the world to Mary and me. During his first three years his sponsors were Brent and Morgan Cornstubble, both professors at West Point. Josh fell in love with them both, including their cats. His last year there as a "firstie," his sponsor was Sergeant Cooper and his family. We continue to stay in touch with both families.

Morgan Cornstubble said, "What stands out to me more than anything else was his big grin and positive attitude. He was always the one to laugh things off or joke around, even when they were plebes and under so much stress. One night over at the house during plebe year, we asked him how things were going, and he told us he had been made to haze himself. 'What did you say?' I asked. 'Well, Ma'am, I just stared myself down and told myself how I wasn't fit to be here and that I was a disgrace. I answered myself, 'Yes, Sir!' Then I made myself drop and do push-ups.' I know there was more; he went on and on about the tongue-lashing he had given himself, and the rest of us were in stitches."

Graduation day arrived in all its glory. A day we had all looked forward to but at the same time dreaded. All of the class of 1996 were beside themselves with excitement. West Point has a whole week of activities leading up to the great day when they get to throw their hats in the air. I walked around all week in an excited fog of unbelief. I know I had pride gushing out all over. As new cadets in 1992, Josh and his classmates repeated a solemn oath to support the Constitution out on that plain beside the Hudson River. And on June 1, 1996, they made another oath, which was to support and defend the Constitution. Then the hats flew. I cannot begin to describe the feelings I myself experienced that day. I stood in Michie Stadium and was overwhelmed with the privilege to stand there among so many men and women with so much character and honor, committed to protecting our freedom. I have always felt safe but from that moment on, I declared to never worry about our country's ability to keep us safe. We had the beautiful opportunity that day to be a part of something that was indescribable. There stood the prime cut of our national defense full of duty, honor, and country. That's who heroes are…

After the ceremony, we proceeded to find a private area for our family and friends to witness Josh getting "pinned" with his lieutenant bars. His grin said it all. A cadet can choose anyone who is a member of the military to present their rank to them. It is someone who is special. The Cornstubbles were no longer at West Point during Josh's senior year so his sponsor was Sergeant Al Cooper and his lovely family. Josh truly loved the Cooper family and became very close to them. I remember Josh calling home after being at West Point for a year or so and said, "Dad, I found the secret to being a successful officer." I immediately questioned how he could know that after only being there for a short time. He said, "I have learned to be good to my sergeant and he will take care of me." Josh showed us the wisdom of that statement time and time again when he entered the army for service. Josh loved Sergeant Cooper and became so close to his family that he asked him to pin on his bars after graduation. It was a very unusual thing to do as most of the cadets had a professor who was an officer or a leadership officer at West Point do the honors. Josh continued with the same attitude with his sergeants when he became an officer and it made all the difference. Because of relying on the one who really runs the men, Josh had the utmost respect from those under him. It was understood he was their superior but he was also their friend. As I recall those four years Josh spent at West Point from "R" day to graduation, I understand a little of the faith he showed that I have spoken of earlier. I am not saying it was easy, but Josh made it look that way. That is what heroes do…and Josh kept moving forward.

An entry in one of Josh's journals during his time at West Point:

The Road Not Taken
by Robert Frost

Two roads diverged in a yellow wood,
And sorry I could not travel both
And be one traveler, long I stood
And looked down one as far as I could
To where it bent in the undergrowth;

Then took the other, as just as fair,
And having perhaps the better claim,
Because it was grassy and wanted wear,
Though as for that, the passing there
Had worn them really about the same,

And both that morning equally lay
In leaves no step had trodden black.
Oh, I kept the first for another day!
Yet knowing how way leads on to way,
I doubted if I should ever come back.

I shall be telling this with a sigh,
Somewhere ages and ages hence;
Two roads diverged in a yellow wood, and I—
I took the one less traveled by,
And that has made all the difference.

"I daily subject myself to the complete control of the gray walls surrounding me, and it is by choice that I sacrifice my freedom. I do not do it in pursuit of money, or power, nor do I make the sacrifices in pursuit of a dream. It is something deeper, more rare, and more precious than any of these motives can foster. It is the pursuit of glory that drives my soul in the chase to capture this goal that few actually attain. On the road to achieving this life-long quest, a man's character is forged into shape like steel—beaten and put into the fire until the impurities are gone and all that is left is a will of cold and unbending strength. As Frost so eloquently reflected, 'I took the one less traveled by, And that has made all the difference.'"

--Cadet Joshua T. Byers, 1993
USMA, Class of 1996

The Apostle Paul said in 2 Corinthians 4:8-9 NLT: "We are pressed on every side by troubles, but we are not crushed. We are perplexed, but not driven to despair. We are hunted down, but never abandoned by God. We get knocked down, but we are not destroyed." (NLT)

It is such an amazing reality in my limited life experiences that I realize a real hero is "...knocked down but not knocked out." That's what heroes do...

"Today is your day and mine, the only day we have, the day in which we play our part. What our part may signify in the great whole, we may not understand; but we are here to play it, and now is our time."
- David Starr Jordan

CHAPTER SIX

DEPLOYED TO WAR

"Deliver me, O Lord, from evil men; preserve me from
violent men, who plan evil things in their heart and stir
up wars continually." Psalm 140:1-2 ESV

As we study God's Word, we find war is a constant reality. From the
Garden of Eden when Cain and Abel had their differences, we deal with
an unfortunate choice when problems arise between humans who cannot
get along together. When we study the wars that have been fought down
through the ages and up to the present, the sadness and the result of what
man does to man is almost unbelievable. Our present struggle, which we
find ourselves in at the time of this writing, is the very heart of the biblical
wars described in the Holy Bible.

A real hero always considers how he or she can lead to the very best
of their ability in order to accomplish the mission before them. During
Josh's tank training at Fort Knox, Kentucky he approached his superiors
to allow him to attend Ranger School. If one chooses to branch infantry
in the army, they are allowed automatically to try and finish Ranger
training. Josh chose to branch Armor therefore, he had to be selected for
Ranger School. If the soldier can complete this grueling, almost impossible
training (in Josh's class only 12 out of the 63 that started in his class
graduated) they receive the admired and sought after Ranger Tab.

Josh was selected and excitingly called to tell us. I could not understand
why in the world he would want to subject himself to such horrific physical
and mental treatment. My hat goes off to those who are Rangers as well
as to anyone who goes the extra mile to be in one of our military's special

forces. "Why do you choose this unnatural beating after going through all the other difficult training you have done? I think it is adding insult to injury." I will never forget Josh's answer when I asked. "Dad." he said. "When I become a commander, or even before that as an officer, I want my soldiers to know I have been trained the best I can be. I want them to be assured of my leadership no matter the cost I have to pay." That is what heroes do…

In 1997 when Josh was stationed at Fort Stewart, Georgia, we were serving as church planters on Hilton Head Island, South Carolina, so having Josh within an hour of us was a wonderful thing. It was a blessing after being so far apart for years to be able to visit with Josh without much traveling involved. Jared, at 15, really wanted a dog and Josh wanted to accommodate his brother. He had really missed Jared's early teen years, and decided to buy him a bulldog mix puppy. That is when Winston (part American, and part English bulldog) became a part of the family. Jared had the usual busy teen life; therefore, Winston and I became inseparable.

In 1998 we moved to Habersham County, Georgia, to plant another church. God truly blessed our work there as we witnessed a viable, excited group of people wanting to continue God's work in that part of God's creation. In December of that year, Josh married the love of his life, Kim, in a beautiful church in Clarkesville, Georgia.

As I fast forward to 2001, it was a usual Tuesday morning in September and my daily routine included a trip to the Post Office for Winston and me. Winston had his window down and was enjoying his favorite thing in all the world; biting the air. After the Post Office stop, for which I noticed the flag at half-mast and wondered who died, I went to the hardware store to pick up a bolt I needed. When I walked in, my world was forever changed. The many Televisions in the entrance of the store were broadcasting the World Trade Center buildings falling down. It was 9/11.

We were full of anxiety, as would be expected with a child in the military, for we had been attacked by the enemy on our own soil. How could that happen? Who wasn't watching or guarding? We had so many questions and were full of frustration just as many others were. The last time this had occurred was at Pearl Harbor in December 1941. After Josh served his three years at Fort Stewart, he was sent to Fort Leonard Wood, Missouri, to continue his education. During his time there, he earned a Masters in Civil Engineering from the University of Missouri, Rolla. He was then transferred to Fort Carson, Colorado, in 2001 to begin his tour with the 2nd Battalion, 3rd Armored Cavalry Division to become company commander, which he had often said was his goal since West Point days. We immediately tried to call Josh, but he was on a "lock down" at Fort Carson and on alert for days.

Josh had recently become the interim aide to the commanding general and was to serve in that position the first few weeks after the new general came in to be the commanding general. We finally made contact with Josh and were assured that the best army in the world was ready and anxious to engage the enemy. Following that dreadful day, I saw patriotism at it's best. Josh wanted to go and protect his country immediately, so did many young men and women who readily volunteered to serve our great country. I saw patriotism in almost every American's house where the least display was a single American flag, but many had several flags and other displays.

Josh would go to protect our freedom after the attack on Afghanistan in October of 2001, as most of the military would. After he served as aide-de-camp for General "Hondo" Campbell, the commanding general of Fort Carson, for a little over a year, he prepared to deploy to Iraq. President George W. Bush had declared war on dictator, Saddam Hussein. In March of 2003, Josh left for the Arab country of Iraq to win the war on terrorism. He was with the 2nd Battalion, 3rd Armored Cavalry Division who was deployed to join the 3rd Infantry Division to take control of Iraq and stop the terrorist group, Al Qaeda.

In December of 2002, Josh and his wife Kim came to visit for Christmas. We did not know that would be his last visit. The last time we would see him alive, on this earth, was when we took them to the Atlanta Airport the first week of January 2003 on their return to Colorado. (Ironically, the same place we would hear the awful news that Josh had been killed.) I remember hugging good-bye and watching as he and Kim disappeared in the distance. I remember he was sure to look up as they went through security to wave good-bye. He signed to us in American Sign Language the "I love you" sign as he slipped from our sight. That was the last time I saw my son alive. He wore his usual smile that will forever be with me; but he also had a knowing look that this may be the last time to see us on this earth. We know we will see him again one day in Heaven. I often revisit our airport good-bye and think about if I had known that was it, what more would I have said? We talked to him often after he received his orders to deploy, and even checked on flights to Colorado before he left. He insisted that even if we made the trip, he could not spend any time with us since they were working 17-hour days to prepare. The last time I heard his voice was when he called just before leaving the states for Iraq. He assured me that he was in God's will, and would be safer in a war torn country of Iraq than if he was on a beach somewhere sipping lemonade. As I hung up the phone I thought, "What a man, ready for whatever may come, all to protect my freedom and the freedom of every American." There are no words for how proud I was of him that day, and everyday.

Two of Josh's best friends who served with him in Iraq were Captain James Dayhoff and Captain Jesse Sellars. They were inseparable as a team as well as comrades. Jesse escorted Josh's body home for burial. We've heard many stories about their time in Iraq. I want to share a few of those. CPT James Dayhoff shares about a time when they had not been in Iraq very long:

> **Somehow, our squadron decided to park our TOC (Tactical Operations Center) next to a humongous ammunition site that the locals were looting for wood and other stuff. Within days, it was ablaze from cigarette ashes dropped by the looters. On day 4, it exploded. The boom was large enough to knock nearly everyone down in the TOC. Next thing we knew, rockets and other projectiles were slamming the ground around the TOC and one hit the building we had occupied. In quick order, we hauled ass across the compound to escape. I remember running down a corridor or tight alley, when Josh and Jesse stopped and were looking up. I could see a rocket or missile flying straight up in the air, maybe 1000 feet high, then it turned toward the earth. The three of us jigged back and forth across the path trying to decide which way to go as it came down toward us – or at least it appeared to be. It actually landed quite a way from us. Later, after things calmed down, we were sitting on a sidewalk talking about happened, when the ammo dump exploded again. Before I could think, Josh had me off the ground and against the wall behind us. I don't remember moving. I asked how I had gotten there and Josh said, "I don't know." Jesse said, "Josh yanked you off the sidewalk and threw you against the wall." It was at least 20 feet between the two. Debris was starting to fall all over the place by then. We moved the TOC shortly after that.**

This is probably the funniest thing I ever heard Josh say. A few weeks into our deployment, Josh, Jesse, and I were taking a short break one evening and chatting on the upper deck of the control tower we had occupied. We were looking over Al Fallujah and Al Habbanyah. We were talking about plans, I think. Out of nowhere, Josh says, "You know what I don't get? How the hell did civilization start here? Let's say I am traveling across the wilderness and looking for a great place to live. So, I stop here? You'd think God would have told me it was only a couple hundred more miles – you know?" Since arriving in Iraq, I hadn't laughed so hard – hard enough, the SCO sent someone to quiet us.

There isn't a day that goes by that I don't wish that one of my trucks hadn't broken down that fateful day and I'd have gone before Josh. That morning the order of march was my unit (Lion), then Fox, then the rest of the squadron. The battery was tasked with FOB (forward operating base) security, so we had to get there first. Just as I was about to leave the FOB in Ramadi, one of my trucks scored a coolant leak. I called up to squadron and told them I would be late. Shortly after that, Josh called up and requested to move. His request was granted (he did have Lieutenant Colonel Hickey with him). I listened on the radio in my truck to the events that unfolded over the next hour, to my horror. I don't even know if Jesse (Captain Jesse Sellars) knows this, I haven't even told Mira (James's wife). Just as Josh rolled out, he came across the radio (he knew I was flaming mad, for missing SP [security patrol]) and said, "Lion 6 this is Fox 6, I'm rollin' man...I'll see you when you get there." I replied with, "Okay, roger. Be safe." I am angry, hurt, lost, bewildered, and answerless. I don't know if things would have been different if I would have gone first... if I would have been hit. I have always wondered, what if I'd have been in the same place in the convoy, the same seat as Josh.

When Josh closed his eyes in death that day, he was about the 300th of our military personnel to give their lives in personal sacrifice for our great country in this present conflict. Our military is the greatest in the world. We, civilians, often go about our day thinking of how busy we are, of all the things we have to do, often feeling sorry for ourselves when there is a soldier faithfully standing in the gap. One who is going without food, rest, and very little sleep, often not in succession but in short increments here and there throughout their day. These sacrifices aren't for a high salary but because of patriotism and for a love of their country. You have heard the familiar saying, "Freedom is not free." It not only costs our country's best men and women their lives, but soldiers who do come back with their lives are injured in many other ways. Some have lost limbs among other physical and emotional needs. Every military individual serving in hostile territory comes home having been affected in some way. Several of Josh's friends have gone through full-blown P.T.S.D. (post traumatic stress disorder) and have experienced hell on earth. The trauma of leaving friends who were killed, witnessing things that no man should see, and dealing with the hurts of war that only those who have faced it understand. One effect of P.T.S.D. is feeling completely dead inside. They leave the battlefield with the burden of loneliness, nothing mentally left to give, and lost emotions. They feel the loss of self-worth. This has contributed to the largest number of suicides in the history of our country's military forces. Some return with T.B.I. (traumatic brain injury), which deals with the actual episodes of loud noises such as the many explosions they experienced. All of our country's best deal with some amount of combat stress by having returned from such horror. "Freedom is not Free" includes not only those who lost their lives, or returned with injuries, but the families who suffer due to death, victims of emotional hurts, and the reality that their loved ones have faced such horrific things. In fact, my wife, our two sons, and I have dealt with "secondary" P.T.S.D., which is simply trying to deal with the tragic loss of a loved one. Freedom Is Not Free!

When Josh passed from this life on earth to life eternal with our Heavenly Father, his eyes may have closed to a brutal death; but they opened to eternal life — a place the Bible says is without pain, death, or tears. I am looking forward to seeing our Savior and Josh; but for now, I will continue to shed tears not because of where Josh is but because I miss him every day. If you have lost someone close, then you truly understand.

Plebe Parent Weekend at West Point, March 1993
"My Three Sons"

Pinning the Ranger Tab on Josh, May 1, 1997

Josh on his wedding day –
December 19, 1998

Mail Call in Iraq

Josh, James Dayhoff and Jesse Sellars in Iraq
the day Josh learned that he would become
Fox Troop Commander, June 2003

The Lucky 7: Ben Gardner, Abe Usher, Josh, Chris Masters, Stan Hardee, Doel
Baughman, Mark Miller

Graduation Day at West
Point June 1, 1996

Enjoying a mountain vacation August, 1983

Fountain, Colorado – Liberty Heights Subdivision Street
Sign: Josh Byers Way / Hero Lane

Our last family portrait with Josh April, 2001
Standing: Josh, Kim, Mary, Lloyd
Seated: Milam and Jared

Josh in Kindergarten
Age 5

June 1, 1996 Brothers celebrate Josh's West
Point Graduation

"Leaders are not born. They are made. They are made just like anything else... through hard work!"
-Vince Lombardi

CHAPTER SEVEN

MORE MEMORIES...FROM BATTLE BUDDIES

"There is no greater love than to lay down one's life for one's friends." John 15:13 NLT

Never in all my days, have I seen the closeness of our fellow man as I have witnessed in the bond soldiers have for one another. The slogan for the Army not long ago was "We are an army of ONE." This adamantly describes our military as a team — each one working together to accomplish the mission sent down from above. It is meticulously carried out in a precise manner to reach the objective. As a pastor for over 35 years, I wish the churches I have worked and been involved with would work together like I have witnessed our military do. Our world would be a much better place. I saw this when Josh started West Point, and of course, when he became an officer facing the difficult task of seeing that his men did their jobs. I played football in high school and quickly discovered if the eleven positions don't do their individual assignments, and work as a team, then the team cannot win. I quickly learned from conversations with Josh that each soldier depends on his fellow comrade in every situation when carrying out a mission. I didn't fully understand this bond until we actually lost Josh and began to communicate with those who had served alongside him. The bond of family is built in training and fighting together. I want to share some of my interviews and letters from those who served with Josh.

Major Andrew J. Watson shared this:

> **Josh was an inspiration to so many of us that he
> served with. No matter what the circumstances were,
> he always maintained a positive attitude and was the
> sort of leader that his peers modeled their actions
> after. When Josh was serving as the executive officer
> of HHC, 3-69 AR, his office was a place of refuge for
> many of us serving with him. Being a year behind
> Josh, I was always able to pull up a chair, kick my
> feet up, and bounce questions and ideas off him. Josh
> never failed to listen intently and always offered advice
> or suggestions when it was needed. I last saw Josh the
> night before we all started to head north from Kuwait
> into Iraq, and we wished each other good luck and
> talked briefly of our time together at Fort Stewart
> and plans for the future. As always, he was a model
> of quiet confidence and enthusiasm. Several months
> later, after we were both in command of different
> Squadrons, I was scheduled to link up with Josh and
> assume his battle space in Ar Ramadi. Unfortunately,
> he was killed several days before the scheduled relief
> in place could occur. Several weeks later, I had the
> honor of leading the mission that captured several of
> the insurgents who had planned and participated in
> the ambush where Josh lost his life. It was the least I
> could do for a mentor and a friend who had helped to
> shape me into the soldier I am today.**

Abe Usher was Josh's best friend while at West Point. They were two of "the Lucky Seven," who attended BSU (Baptist Student Union) and became the best of friends. I mentioned them in a previous chapter and again, I marvel at the bond of our country's best. These are the words Abe shared at Josh's funeral.

> **I had the privilege of meeting Josh while we were
> attending West Point together as cadets. He loved the
> Lord Jesus Christ, and he loved his family and friends.
> He was an inspiration to me, and to those who knew
> him. One special characteristic that I remember about**

Josh is that he always knew where he was and where he was going.

I recall when we were in cadet field training, an officer questioned Josh while he was leading a patrol of fellow cadets. The officer asked Josh, "Are you lost cadet?" and he replied "No sir, I've got my pace count and azimuth."

While navigating by foot, pace count and azimuth are two critical measurements. Pace count is the measure of your footsteps. It tells how far you have come and how far you have to go.

In his relationship with God, Josh kept his pace count and azimuth straight. Josh measured his footsteps by the Word of God, and he kept his eyes fixed on Jesus Christ for his direction. I witnessed Josh's marvelous faith in his life as a cadet, as a soldier, and as a family man.

I met Josh Byers in June of 1992 and he instantly became my best friend at West Point. I was drawn to him because of his love for Jesus Christ. I spent much time with Josh, studying academics, lifting weights, exercising, studying the Bible, and praying. Josh continually prayed for me, encouraged me, and challenged me. Josh subordinated his goals to serve others. He volunteered his time to Special Olympics and community events at West Point. He also served as a lay leader in the Baptist church there. In his cadet ring, Josh had an inscription that reads: "To Lead is to Serve." He followed Jesus Christ's example of servant leadership, and he sought to glorify God in all of his efforts. Josh was known for his upright character; his classmates selected him to serve as the executive officer of the Cadet Honor Committee, a very high distinction at West Point. Serving as a leader of the honor code was natural for him because the fruit of the Holy Spirit was so evident in his life. Our last week together at West Point, Josh and I attended a Promise Keepers conference in Washington, DC. At that conference Josh shared his faith and led a man to Christ. In our

West Point yearbook, under Josh's picture there is a reference to the scripture Joshua 1:9: "Have I not commanded you? Be strong and courageous! Do not tremble or be dismayed, for the Lord your God is with you wherever you go."

As a soldier, Josh was head and shoulders above his peers. He loved his soldiers, and cared for them deeply. He sought every opportunity to make himself the best possible leader for his men. Josh was an Airborne Ranger, and he embodied the Ranger Creed in his actions. Part of the Ranger Creed says, "Never shall I fail my comrades. I will always keep myself mentally alert, physically strong, and morally straight, and I will shoulder more than my share of the task whatever it may be and then some." Indeed Josh was strong for his fellow soldiers. There are several accounts from soldiers in the 3rd ACR that Josh Byers had saved their lives. In his correspondence, Josh often quoted Philippians 4:13, "I can do all things through Christ who strengthens me."

Josh wrote to me in a letter, "I have grown so much closer to the Lord through this experience than I could have ever imagined before actually being in the combat zone. God's presence is so real, His protection so complete. I rely on Him completely everyday and just do my best to perform every task to the best of the ability that He has given me. I also pray for daily wisdom and strength as I lead these incredible soldiers through these times. I have to be strong for them, no matter what; my relationship with Christ is what allows me to do that, day in and day out." Josh led by example and set a high standard for others to follow. He risked his life multiple times to protect the lives of his fellow soldiers and the lives of Iraqi civilians.

Josh's faith was also illustrated in his family relationships. He frequently mentioned his parents and brothers to me at West Point, and asked me to pray for them often. I will never forget December 19, 1998, when Josh married his very best friend, Kim.

It was a beautiful day, to witness the wedding of two such wonderful people. Every time I heard from Josh after his wedding, he made mention of Kim and what a blessing she was to him. In a letter I received from him this past March, he wrote, "Thank you so much for your thoughts, prayers, and concerns for Kim as well. I think she has it harder than me in so many ways. At least I know what's going on here and can do everything in my power to control the danger and understand the risks. She has to sit at home and just wonder, not knowing exactly what I'm doing or when I'm doing it. I pray for her constantly and thank God that He has blessed me with such a wonderful wife. She is not only my wife, but my best friend – I am truly blessed."

Throughout his life, Josh Byers kept his pace count and azimuth. He always measured his steps by the Word of God, and he kept his direction by fixing his eyes on Jesus Christ for his salvation, we are confident that he is now in God's presence in Heaven. I do not know why God chose to take Josh so soon; I will miss him every day for the rest of my life.

I look forward to the day when we will be reunited together in Heaven through the saving grace of Jesus. Until that day, I will seek to remember Josh and honor his memory by living as he lived, measuring my footsteps by the Word of God, keeping my eyes fixed on Jesus Christ, our great hope and salvation.

The following was sent to us in an e-mail. I have been amazed at the number of e-mails we received when Josh was KIA (Killed In Action), from people we had never met, around the world. The writer of this piece is Staff Sergeant Brown whom Josh brought on staff as the General's driver at Fort Carson when he was chosen to be General "Hondo" Campbell's aide. The letter is to an officer he knew who attended church with Josh and Kim when Josh was stationed at Fort Stewart, Georgia.

Sir, I have taken this extremely hard. I found out last night from a friend who thankfully looked me up about CPT Byers. He was my supervisor and friend. I was the CG's (commanding general) driver and he was the aide, we were a three-man team. I was close to Captain Byers and am truly devastated about this. I wish I had been there, maybe I would have spotted something and could have changed things. For more than a year we worked together, he sat at his desk no more than five feet from me. Even though I was a few months older, I looked up to him and respected him not because he was an officer, but because he WAS a True American Soldier to the bottom of his heart and soul. I wish I could have the drive and dedication and pure patriotism that he did. I didn't keep in touch with him after I left Fort Carson, which now I truly regret and will forever. I just figured I would call or e-mail him tomorrow, but tomorrow never came. I thank you for posting that e-mail and I am sharing it with others who are mourning. We spent many late nights and weekends together in our jobs and that bond was strong between us. He was the greatest officer I have ever worked with or known. Always taking care of soldiers and truly dedicated to the Army. Myself and three others are going to be in South Carolina, this Friday and Saturday. CAPTAIN JOSH BYERS means a lot to us and to the Army. I will never forget him and his picture will always be on my wall.

Sergeant First Class Brown wrote the following some time later. He was speaking to Josh. He mentioned that he would be visiting Josh in Laurens, South Carolina. Josh was buried in a country church cemetery; Lisbon Presbyterian Church outside of Laurens, South Carolina. This is my home church and Josh shared with me not long before he passed that if I was still living when he died, that he wanted to be buried in South Carolina. Josh truly loved his home state. He could have been buried in Arlington or West Point, which are the highest honor, but he said that he definitely wanted to be buried "in good ole South Carolina" because that was home.

Hello Captain Byers,
It has been a long time and I think of you often, I
have just returned from Kuwait last December. I am
currently at Fort Gordon attending ANCOC and
graduate 11 Mar. 08. I will be driving out to Laurens
to visit you in a bit. I still think of you a lot and have
had a rough four-and-a-half years being down and
depressed. I am coming out of it and will be at Fort
Huachuca for the next few years, as you know that is
where my family is and where I grew up. I am thinking
of getting the new Bo-flex they have come out with
when I get there. I think of you every time I see a
commercial for it. Well it is about a two-hour drive and
I need to get ready to see you soon, Sir. PS As you see
by the screen name I have been promoted.

Mary and I recently spent a couple of days visiting with Jesse Sellars, his wife Dena and their two boys, Jesse Ray and Carson Joshua. I mentioned Jesse in the previous chapter. He and his precious family live in Colorado Springs, Colorado. They are a beautiful family and made us feel welcome as if we were family. Jesse decided to leave the Army after his 2nd deployment was completed in 2006. After a severe struggle with PTSD and some excellent therapy treatment, Jesse is able to cope even through memories of the past. I wish to note here that Jesse's wife, Dena, has been extremely supportive, which is NOT easy when a loved one experiences the monster that steals the very person we are inside.

Josh and Jesse were very close as they served side by side for several years. It is difficult to imagine what emotions a soldier experiences when a fellow soldier is killed. After spending time with Josh's fellow soldiers I've learned that inadequacy is the immediate demon they deal with. They feel as though they could have prevented the death. We call that type of emotional trauma "survivor's guilt." They have to grieve quickly as they need to keep moving forward and finish the mission. We often fail to realize a soldier's dedication to duties.

Colonel Hickey and the leadership agreed that Jesse would bring Josh home to be buried. He faithfully stayed with Josh's remains until they landed at Dover AFB in Delaware; the national morgue for our military. After Jesse arrived, he soon departed for Fort Carson, Colorado to speak at the memorial service as well as the funeral in South Carolina. Our military takes care of a soldier, they never leave the body until he or she is buried, and they are treated with tremendous care and respect. They immediately assigned another soldier, Captain Luis Montalvan, (who was injured later that year in Iraq and now suffers the scars of war) to be with Josh when Jesse left him. Josh was escorted to South Carolina, to be buried with full military honors. America has the best Army in the world. I pray you understand that and grow daily in appreciation of what they do.

The following words are from Jesse.

> Before I could begin to possibly tell the stories about Josh that I am blessed with, it's very important that you understand the impact that this great American has had on my life. Josh Byers is without a doubt the single greatest American I have ever met. People often say that after a death time heals and that time makes things better. I don't believe this is true, and I certainly do not believe this is the case with Josh. Time doesn't heal, time simply makes it easier to focus on the positive memories and happy moments that you were able to share with that individual. As time increases from the moment of Josh's death his loss has gotten no easier for me. In fact, the sacrifice that was made on behalf of Josh's family on behalf of our nation and on behalf of everyone who loved Josh has only grown more clear and more profound. As time increases the clarity with which I am able to look back on the fond memories that I had with Josh, his influence on my life also grows stronger. I think of Josh every single day, multiple times a day. This is why I strongly believe that Josh's profound impact on my life only grows with intensity as time goes on. And with that, I would like to share some of my fondest memories of Josh to offer a glimpse at why this wonderful man continues to influence my life in so many ways.
>
> The first time that I met Josh must have been in late September or early October of 2002. I was working in the plans operations shop of Sabre Squadron Third Armored Cavalry Regiment; 3rd ACR. Before Josh even arrived to the unit word had spread about his

good reputation. It was kind of a joke in the office because we were the plans and operations office and we had a guy with the last name of Sellars in charge of operations and a guy with the last name of Byers that was going to be in charge of the plans portion of the office. So naturally people began calling it purchasing and sales instead of plans and operations.

When I actually met Josh was at an officer's call at Jack Quinn's Bar and Grill. I didn't know what Josh looked like; so even though he was in the bar, I had no clue that he was there. So I was actually standing close to Josh for some time not knowing exactly who he was. I'm making small talk with some of the guys that were around as the more formal proceedings of the evening began to happen.

As the evening went on, they began to call up to the front all of the new people that were coming to the unit and eventually Josh's name was called. Josh walked up to the front for the first time. I thought, "Okay, so that's Josh Byers." After they had introduced him and welcomed him to the unit they gave him a sheet of stickers that had the unit logo on it. Josh left the front of the room where the formal stuff was going on and came back to stand directly beside me at the bar with that sheet of stickers. I introduced myself and let him know that we would be working in the office together. I also probably made some kind of joke about it. Josh's penetrating smile immediately came out with this southern drawl as he spoke. He smirked as he held up his stickers and he said, "Hey, wanna go put all the stickers on the Regimental Head Quarter's vehicles tomorrow?" This immediately made me laugh and we both had an instant connection with each other.

As time went on and we worked closer and closer together, the more I learned about Josh the more I liked him. I believe it was within five minutes of starting the conversation at the Hail and Farewell that he let me know that his brothers were in a rock band. It was also within the first week that he had brought in a CD of

Bleach and played it for everyone in the office. Before he played this CD I think everyone in the office simply thought, "Okay so your brothers are in a band." We didn't realize exactly how great they were. The smile on Josh's face as it just dawned on everyone of how great these guys are is still an impression on my mind. He just sat there with this big goofy grin as everyone's jaws dropped as they realized these guys are really good. Josh just smiled and shook his head up and down. As he showed us the song with his name in it, he grabbed his Bleach belt buckle from up underneath his BDU (battle dress uniform) uniform top and, flashing it around, said, "That's rock'n roll baby! That's rock'n roll."

Typically, out of all the guys in the office during that time, Josh and I were usually the first two to arrive in the morning and the last two to leave in the evening. This pretty much equated to us getting there when it was dark and us leaving when it was dark. One day when we were leaving the office at night-- it must've been close to eight o'clock -- as we were walking out Josh looks at me and says, "you want to know how I decompress before I get home whenever I leave here so late?" And because he had yet again that smirk and mischievous smile on his face I couldn't help but respond with great anticipation that "yes, I absolutely" did want to know. Josh looks at me and says, "I like to get a little fish tail on the way out of the parking lot." We all parked in a dirt parking lot across the street from our office and there was a dirt road of about one-tenth of a mile long getting out of the dirt parking lot onto the paved street that left Fort Carson. So I watched Josh crawl into his truck, shut the door, turn the lights on and then as he pulled away I could see these red lights swaying back and forth as he cut fish tails getting out of the parking lot. This is something that may seem small to most people, but you have to understand that this is not something that would be typical of an army officer and certainly would not be typical of an officer who was as talented and professional as Josh had been throughout the rest of the day. There were many, many nights when I would pause and wait around just one or two brief moments after Josh left just so I could see his taillights fishtail out of the parking lot. It always made me laugh.

Another great memory that I have of Josh was one day in November when it had snowed overnight the night before. Josh and I had both shown up early before Fort Carson made the call that there was going to be a snow delay for PT (physical training). We got to the office in our PT uniforms and everything was covered in snow and there were no troops around, so I told Josh to come with me to go sledding that morning for PT. Josh hesitated and he said, "I don't know if we should do that." I told him it would be fine and that most of the Joe's were on a PT delay anyway. What Josh was concerned about was going off and playing while others would be having to work. This was the result of his profound dedication to the guys. But I was able to convince him that everybody else was at home sipping hot cocoa waiting for the roads to get better, so it was not going to hurt anything if he went along with me. So finally, he gave in and we grabbed a couple of sleds and went off searching for a sledding hill near Fountain, Colorado. Not too far from Josh's house we found a real long hill that was part of a housing development project. It only snowed about a quarter of an inch there in Fountain, so it was just enough to cover the ground. It was not enough to add any real amount of padding or even an appropriate amount of snow to sled in. But we didn't let that stop us. We walked up to the top of this hill and up to this point I think that Josh still had some level of reservation, but the first time that we got on that sled and headed down that hill on just a bunch of wet dirt and gravel Josh's concerns completely went away. He got that wonderful smile again from ear to ear and you could not have beat it off of his face with a stick. For the rest of the time that was allowed for PT that morning, which must've been probably 45 minutes to an hour, we continued to walk up that hill and sled down on dirt and gravel. We actually thrashed our PT uniforms and the bottom of our sled was completely shredded. We were both laughing out loud and smiling from ear to ear. Kim told me a few days later when I spoke with her that Josh walked in covered in mud and absolutely ecstatic and he made some comment to the effect of "this is how rednecks sled" and laughed and chuckled.

At that time we were all preparing for war. The war had not kicked off yet, and we did not know when it was going to but we knew it was looming. We were in the middle of writing legitimate war plans, lining out our procedures for if we went to war, as well as training to go to war, so this was a very busy time in the shop and it was also a very stressed time because of the long hours. And of those personalities, Josh's was by far the most pleasantly dominating personality in the room. Josh, without a doubt, brought all of us together when there were differences. He made us laugh when things were stressful, and regardless of how much work we had he always seemed to find time to work on the personal relationships. It was during these long workdays that we got to know each other really well. It was also during these workdays that he expressed his dedication to his wife not only through words but also through actions. He expressed his love for his parents as he detailed some of the more humorous moments of growing up, and he expressed his love for his brothers and the rock 'n roll that they produced.

One of the trips that we had taken together as officers was to Fort Lewis, Washington. This trip was designed as a big battle simulation. In this type of simulation there are no troops moving around the battlefield; you have a series of computers that are linked that simulates the battle and the only real functioning human piece of it is the staff. We were staff officers at the time and this required us to go up to

Washington for a couple of weeks and go through this exercise. It was during this exercise that my admiration for Josh certainly grew, and also our friendship grew. We had all gone out to some greasy spoon diner one night. And although there were probably ten or so officers that wound up in this diner going through similar circumstances having similar personalities and getting along really well, Josh spent the majority of that evening talking to a complete stranger about NASCAR. Josh did not even really like NASCAR that much; and he confessed to us after we left the diner that he didn't even really know that much about NASCAR -- only a couple of the driver's names. But as we left that smirk came out again and Josh looked at us and said, "It's good to keep in touch with the real people" and chuckled.

My youngest son is named after Josh.

Mary and I recently had the privilege of visiting Dean Lockhart and his beautiful family in El Paso, Texas. Dean was the scout (the soldier manning the machine gun) in the Humvee Josh was riding in at the time of the explosion. When the IED (improvised explosive device) was ignited, Dean was the only other one in the vehicle severely wounded. The interpreter, who was sitting directly behind Josh on the right side where the force of the blast occurred, was also killed. However, he did live for several hours (this was his first day on the job as Josh's interpreter).

Dean did not immediately lose consciousness. He thought he had been shot in the back but soon learned the reality of the explosion, and he knew he was hurt but not the full extent of his severe injuries. They would not let him see Josh, who had passed away immediately from his shrapnel wounds. He soon went into a comatose state during the transport to the field hospital via helicopter and then on to Landstul, Germany, where he received treatment for crushed bones and pelvis, and severe injuries to his intestines and other organs. His pelvic area and legs have been built back with titanium, and he is a walking miracle. When the shrapnel is released by the power of the explosives inside the IED it is one of the most powerful and useful weapons used by our enemy.

Personally, I believe it is the most cowardly way to fight. But this is war, and we have the best fighting force in the world. They know there is not a chance to overpower us in battle. The shrapnel inside the IED sometimes includes dirty rusty nails, barbed wire, pieces of jagged metal, and anything lethal, wrapped tightly in explosives.

During Dean's three months in Germany, he went from Landstul AFB to a German hospital because this hospital was medically able to deal with the brain damage (yes, I failed to mention that he also had shrapnel in his head). They drilled a hole in the front part of his skull to relieve pressure so the swelling would go down. When Dean was there, no one spoke English and there was no military liaison. His wife Lisa was not able to get there as soon as she had hoped due to awaiting a passport for the new baby she had delivered 13 days earlier. Dean woke up confused after arriving there and was unable to look at himself in a mirror. All he saw were the messed up bones and flesh below his waist. Confused about where he was with no one to communicate in his language, the medical personnel seemed to be taking liberties where he was injured and he could not understand they were merely trying to treat his wounds. He was desperate to get out of there, no matter the cost to his health. He became a "trouble maker" to the staff and was tied to the bed. He did not know the extent of his injuries and it seemed to him, a death sentence. He was confused and his thinking was irrational. Dean thought that he was dead and was in purgatory. It made perfect sense – he was alone, in pain and hopeless. What a blessing when his wife Lisa arrived to help and helped him understand what was happening. The German medical staff did not demonstrate care and respect to him, but they did treat his severe condition with the best of care, medically speaking. He took the long flight back to the United States when he was well enough to be transferred to Walter Reed Hospital in Washington, D.C.

The same officers who knocked on Kim's door to deliver the tragic news also traveled to Lisa's home to inform her of her husband's severe injuries. They explained that due to the type of explosion and the damage done by the shrapnel, Dean most likely would not survive.

The Army would send her and their 13-day-old daughter, Morgan, to be with Dean in Germany. At first, Lisa was told she would have to go alone but being the strong-willed army wife that she is, she saw to it that Morgan also went. The passport for Morgan was delayed because her eyes needed to be open for the picture. This took longer than expected, but they finally got the go ahead. This was just the beginning of a long and difficult journey for Lisa and her family.

We were told by several soldiers how ecstatic Josh became when Morgan was born. He found out that Dean's wife was in labor and went to work finding a satellite phone for Dean to talk with Lisa throughout the remaining part of her labor and birth. Josh loved children and was looking forward to starting a family with Kim after returning from this deployment. He told us in that last phone call before he left U.S. soil that he was going to make us grandparents soon after his return.

Thanks to our Father in Heaven who performs miracles, the Lockhart family is now doing great and still serving in the U.S. Army. Dean will soon be promoted to sergeant major. They were given another miracle in 2006, just three years after the tragedy with the birth of their daughter, Elizabeth. Dean was told that it would be impossible for him to father another child after his injuries.

Forty days before he was deployed to Heaven Josh was put in command of Fox Troop in the 3rd Armored Cavalry Division. Forty days is a significant amount of time in God's Word. Ross Bryan, who served under Josh's command recently shared these words with Mary and me. It is no coincidence that we received this as I was completing my book. He wrote:

> *Of course I have some wonderful memories of Captain Byers! First allow me to offer my condolences for your loss. He was a man of the highest caliber and an all-around excellent leader. He's greatly missed by those who had the pleasure of serving with him. My earliest memories of Josh are in the passion he displayed in training us up in the month before our deployment. He and one of his counterparts in Sabre Squadron led a bottom-up effort to make sure that all dismounted squads were adequately trained in the proper methodology of Military Operations in Urban Terrain and Close Quarters Combat. Up until then, the majority of our training in the Cav was grounded in conventional battlefield warfare, as seen during the first Gulf War and all too common throughout the Cold War. In retrospect, our training regimen wasn't consistent with what we'd later encounter in the mean streets of Iraq. As someone who'd been through Ranger school and was well schooled in military history, Josh had a firm grasp as to what kind of fighting we might encounter. I can't help but think that the superb training he gave us helped to*

save lives. Because of his persistence and dedication, the whole of Sabre Squadron went into battle much better prepared. What a difference one person can make!

Months later, everyone in Fox was delighted to hear that Captain Byers would be taking over command of our troop. He was genuinely liked by the men, and that's not something all officers can say. Sometimes enlisted folks don't jive well with those in the officer corps. So when everyone heard we'd be getting Byers, it came as a huge relief! Upon taking over the reins for Fox, he made it a top priority to meet with each platoon and learn the name of every soldier he'd be leading. He'd regularly walk around our makeshift billets in an almost shepherdly fashion, checking on each of his soldiers. I got pretty used to him strolling up to my cot and jovially greeting me with, "What's up, Stud?" It's not always easy for commanders to connect with their troops, especially during the mid-point of a rough deployment, but for Josh it came quite naturally. I remember him as being a lead-from-the-front kind of CO who liked to be fully involved in every major operation.

But there are two memories in particular that will remain forever ingrained in the collective memory of every Fox trooper who served under him:

By mid-summer, morale was a bit low. The heat was unbearable, people were getting homesick, our living conditions hadn't improved much, and there was much speculation as to when we'd be going home. So Josh took it upon himself to liven things up that July 4th by throwing this big Independence Day shindig that wound up being a real hoot. Seven years later it's all kind of a blur for me now, but I remember patrols were light that day and spirits were high. We had a barbeque pit, lots of cold soda and watermelon, and yes, live chickens that'd been bought for the sole purpose of a late afternoon chicken race! And at the center of this Fox Troop carousel was Josh, the gathering's mad genius bent on seeing to it that we had a great time and managed to forget for a day that we were seven-thousand miles from home.

Second on the list of these fond memories we share was the evening of July 22, just hours before that fateful mission *for which he gave his life. Any grunt who's ever served in Iraq knows he can always expect his living conditions to be far below par until his final days at any given location; out of nowhere MWR centers suddenly spring up, electricity and internet becomes accessible, air-conditioners are trucked in, and one's left wondering where the hell all of this wonderful stuff was months earlier! So was the case with Fox Troop, who finally got some of these accommodations just a few days before our big move back to Fallujah. That Tuesday evening, all of us squeezed into a small room on the first floor of our living quarters to watch the movie "Old School." We roared with laughter at every scene, especially halfway through the film when Will Ferrell's character, "Frank," bellows out in anguish over the loss of his dear friend and fellow pledge, "Blue," yelling the old man's name aloud at his funeral. "You're my boy, Blue!" Josh howled at the top of lungs, echoing Ferrell's line, which only caused us all to laugh that much harder.*

After the movie, whereas most of our guys bedded down for one of their last nights in Ramadi, our crew barely got a wink of sleep before we started gearing up for one of our final missions there. Early that Wednesday morning, we hit the streets in the hours just before daybreak, and got back sometime around breakfast. I grounded my gear in the vehicle, grabbed something to snack on, and raced upstairs to catch a little shuteye.

I passed Josh, who greeted me with his usual "What's up, Stud?" as I dashed up the stairwell.

"Not much, Sir." I replied. I wanted to stop and chat with him, but he was getting ready for his leader's reconnaissance to Fallujah – a necessary preclusion to our unit's scheduled move the following day. Before I knew it, I was passed out on my cot. Then suddenly I felt someone shaking my arm. That's when I heard the news. I couldn't believe then, and still have a hard time believing that so many of these wonderful young men I served with are gone.

Well, I suppose I've written enough. And again, allow me to offer my most heartfelt condolences. You're all very blessed

> *to have had someone like Josh in your life, as are we who had*
> *the honor of serving under him. Take care and God bless.*
> *Brave Rifles!*
> *-Ross Bryan*

These great men who shared their memories and a host of army buddies who fought the fight with total commitment are "moving forward"! We are so very blessed and privileged to be associated with these dedicated Americans. They are real heroes…

The following are lyrics from the song, "Andy's Doin' Time" written by Bleach soon after 9/11. It mentions Josh and our dog, Winston. I include this here because Jesse spoke about how proud Josh was of his brothers and this is the song he played for them at work one day.

Artist: Bleach
Song: Andy's Doing Time
Album: *Again, For The First Time*

Oh no, Andy's doin' time
Mike said his home school's fine
And Jimmy, the job never ends
Now you gotta start again
Mom said that Kathy's great
Look now, cause Angie's stayin' up late with Journey
Shari and Jenn and I'm so glad they're friends

So I move on and on into the sun
You say I'm the lucky one
Am I really the lucky one

Hey Josh, how's the service
All this talk of war makes me nervous
But Deisel is coming to the show
Tell me something I don't know
I know that Winston's the man
If you go in you better hide your hands
I bet that mama's been cookin' something good
I'd head home if I could

But I gotta move on and on into the sun
You say I'm the lucky one
Am I really the lucky one
Am I the lucky one
Yeah the lucky one

Oh Shack, I know money's tight
But man, don't give up the fight

Cause we're moving on and on and on
We'll head out towards the sun
Cause we're the lucky ones
Yeah the lucky ones

I also include the following poem because it is on the monument that was erected at Fort Carson and now moved to Fort Hood memorializing those who died in Iraq from 2/3ACR.

Fiddler's Green

The story of Fiddler's Green was published in 1923, in Cavalry Journal. According to this article, it was inspired by a story told by Captain "Sammy" Pearson at a campfire in the <u>Medicine Bow Mountains</u> of <u>Wyoming</u>. It is still used by modern cavalry units to memorialize the deceased.

Halfway down the trail to Hell,
In a shady meadow green
Are the Souls of all dead troopers camped,
Near a good old-time canteen.
And this eternal resting place
Is known as Fiddlers' Green.
Marching past, straight through to Hell
The Infantry are seen.
Accompanied by the Engineers,
Artillery and Marines,
For none but the shades of Cavalrymen
Dismount at Fiddlers' Green.
Though some go curving down the trail

To seek a warmer scene.
No trooper ever gets to Hell
Ere he's emptied his canteen.
And so rides back to drink again
With friends at Fiddlers' Green.
And so when man and horse go down
Beneath a saber keen,
Or in a roaring charge of fierce melee
You stop a bullet clean,
And the hostiles come to get your scalp,
Just empty your canteen,
And put your pistol to your head
And go to Fiddlers' Green.

"God whispers to us through our pleasures, but he screams at us through our pain. The pain is God's megaphone to the deaf world."
- C.S. Lewis

CHAPTER EIGHT

ATLANTA AIRPORT AND DEATH

by Mary Byers

*"Do not be afraid, for I have ransomed you. I have called
you by name; you are mine. When you go through deep
waters, I will be with you. When you go through rivers of
difficulty, you will not drown. When you walk through the
fire of oppression, you will not be burned up; the flames
will not consume you. For I am the Lord, your God, the
Holy One of Israel, your Savior," Isaiah 43: 1b – 3a NLT*

I often reflect on the days and weeks immediately following Josh's untimely
and shocking death. Strangely some of those thoughts haven't been foremost
in my mind until recently, four years after that life retching day of July
23, 2003. I remember how innocent we were as we came up the escalator
after going through US Customs in the Atlanta Airport. This was going
to be a day of celebration for two reasons: 1. Milam and Ashley had just
gotten engaged two days prior on July 21, 2003. 2. It was my (Mary) 50th
birthday. It's scary how quickly your whole life and perspective can change.
We walked up after finally spotting Milam and Jared in the back of the
crowd of onlookers as we got off the escalator. They looked so unmoved
by our arrival, I immediately asked, "Why are you so solemn?" But, even
then, I rambled on about the engagement and quickly asked where Ashley
was so I could see the ring. About that very moment she walked up, trying

to force a smile but straining to do so. In moments, our innocence was catapulted to horror as Milam put his arms around both Lloyd and me and told us that he had bad news that he needed to share with us. Still, I grasped for the mere hope that it was someone of distant kin or of old age that was either very sick or near death. Never did I allow my mind to even think it could be death and certainly not the death of our oldest son. It was almost like I was in a deep hole as Milam said those horrible words, "Josh died this morning." I think I screamed, "No!" possibly many times, and I felt numb as though my whole body were jelly and would collapse. Lloyd there by my side, began to cry and shake uncontrollably. I immediately felt concern that he would have a stroke or heart attack. He was in total shock. I began to beg, "Please wake me up, this has to be a dream, it can't be true." Jared, Milam and Ashley tried to console us by hugging us and trying to hold the both of us up.

I remember looking at people as they passed by us and wondering how they could be so "normal," untouched by this horrible earth shattering news. Some would stare for a moment but most walked by as if nothing was wrong. They had to see our anguish, but no one stopped to ask if they could help.

We somehow managed after some time, to retrieve our luggage and make our way to the car. We had been delayed 24 hours due to mechanical problems on the plane from Guam to Tokyo. After flying back to Guam and getting another plane, we flew to Tokyo but missed our connection to the mainland. The airline took care of us very well that night in Tokyo and we relaxed, had a delicious meal, and got a good night's sleep in a real bed, not the airline seat that we were supposed to be in for the 14-hour flight from Tokyo to Atlanta. The next morning it was already my birthday in Tokyo as we waited for the time to go to the airport to catch our afternoon flight.

I remember thinking that I would actually have two days of my birthday since we would lose a day in our travels and land in Atlanta on the afternoon of July 23. That was one of my final "good" memories of that birthday.

Just before we boarded the plane, we had gotten a *USA Today* at the gift shop to read on the plane, so Lloyd and I were reading some of it to pass the time. On the front page of the section I was holding there was a picture of a Humvee that had burned after an explosion. I had a horrible pang in my heart as I thought, "That could be Josh." I think that was the first time I had actually allowed myself to go there since Josh had left.

As we left the airport the boys told us that they had asked the hotel where they had stayed the night before to let us use the room for a few extra hours due to our news and having no where to go close by. They had reluctantly agreed and said only until 6 p.m. By the time we got to the hotel it was almost 5 p.m., so we had very little time there.

We began to make phone calls and wondered who nearby could help. It was rush hour in Atlanta so the idea of someone getting to us quickly was totally impossible.

We soon thought about our friends, Tommy and Gerri Sue Fish, who lived in nearby northeast Georgia. We called them and they insisted on meeting us on the east side of Atlanta at a *Cracker Barrel*. We left the airport Hilton and drove to the other side of downtown to meet them.

I began thinking of how horrible it must have been for Milam and Jared to wait those hours between the time they had heard the news of Josh's death from Kim, his wife, until the dreaded time that we arrived at the airport. I can't imagine what they went through. I wish the Army had gotten someone to be there with them, I think it would have helped. The Army thought we were already enroute to South Carolina to Lloyd's mother's home because Kim thought we had arrived on the day before. They were arranging for soldiers to go to NaNa's house to give us the news. After realizing that these soldiers were about to walk up on an 81-year-old-grandmother's steps to give her this terrible news, we called Lloyd's brother-in-law and told him the news and he went immediately up to Lloyd's mother's house along with Lloyd's sister, to give her the news. Moments after getting there and breaking the news to her, the soldiers arrived. It was good that they were there for her and for Lloyd's sister, Gayle, because a chaplain was one of the ones sent and he was able to comfort them and pray with them for some time.

After spending some time with our friends, Tommy and Gerri Sue, we began our long drive back to Nashville, where Milam and Jared were living. It was 1 or 2 a.m. when we arrived and a few of their friends were there to greet and comfort us. We finally went to bed, on an air mattress, in the living room floor of the apartment, about 4:30 a.m. There was little sleep, but we were so exhausted it helped to lie down and rest. We got up early the next morning and began making calls and receiving calls from family and friends who had heard the news. There were also reporters wanting to talk with us about interviews.

A soldier from Fort Campbell called to ask if they could send someone to give us official notice even though they knew that we already had the news. They said he would arrive around 2 p.m. that afternoon. He didn't get there until almost 5 p.m., and when he knocked on the door and we stood there as the door opened; it was still a final blow and somehow a reality hit that this news was indeed true. The soldier was a captain, very much like Josh in his military background. We found ourselves feeling so sorry for him as he struggled to give us the news. Jared especially worried about him afterward and told me that I should call later to check on him.

Friends visited in Nashville for a couple of days, and then we flew to Colorado Springs on Saturday afternoon to be with Kim and prepare for the Memorial Service that would be held there at Fort Carson on the following Wednesday. We were blessed by being given enough miles for our flights to Colorado by General Hondo Campbell. His aide arranged all the tickets for us and this will never be forgotten.

Arriving at Josh and Kim's home was beyond difficult. We had talked to Kim by phone a lot since hearing the news, but to see her, hug her, and cry together was very surreal.

Walking across the threshold of their home was one of the saddest moments I have ever experienced. Going up the few steps to their front porch was like lifting cement when I raised my legs to make each step. All the memories of times there visiting with Josh and Kim and their two Boxers, Reno and Harley, began flooding through my mind. If only I could turn back time and change these events...

The next few days were filled with visits from friends, family, Josh's comrades and their families coming by to visit us. We would recall fun times and memories and be able to laugh but in the next moment tears would come streaming down. It was like an emotional roller coaster.

On the day of the Fort Carson Memorial Service I can recall sitting between Kim and Lloyd there in the Post Chapel looking at the photo of my son and begging God to give me the strength to get through. As eulogies were shared my mind recalled memories of Josh being born, running around as a young child and growing up. The flood of memories was almost unbearable. Finally, at some point I felt a peace come over me and that is what got me through the remainder of the service. I know God was assuring me that He was there with me and that Josh was okay.

We left Colorado the following day, a Thursday, to fly back to Tennessee and then drove to South Carolina the next day for the visitation that night. The funeral service and burial were on Saturday at a country church and small cemetery there in Josh's beloved home state, South Carolina.

Portions of those first days, weeks and even months are hard to remember and sometimes I feel as if I were on the outside looking in. But we pushed ourselves forward because we knew that was what Josh would want us to do.

All of those times that Josh had a scrape or a cut, I had been there to put the band-aid on and scoop him up in my arms to comfort him but as he grew up and left home, I couldn't be there, I just had to trust that God was there with him. It's so hard as a mother to do this. We know we have to let go but our hearts hold on so tight.

On that fateful day in Iraq, just outside of Ramadi, Josh had a *"boo boo"* and I wasn't there. Oh, if I could have taken that shrapnel from the IED I would have done it a thousand times over. If I had been there I would have thrown myself into the path of that explosion and let my body take it all. But I wasn't there. I will always wonder if he felt the pain, if he knew he was hit, if he knew that he was dying. I know you say, "Why does it matter?" but to me it does. To me I would give anything to know his last thoughts, to hear his last words. But God didn't see fit for that to happen. God was watching Josh. He healed him, kept him safe, protected him, just not the way I had wanted Him to as I prayed all those Mother's prayers for him as I was in Guam after he left for Iraq. God delivered him into eternity and he will never hurt again, never have to say good-bye again. But I'm still here and oh, how I miss him. At times my heart aches and I can hardly breathe. Sometimes it feels just like it just happened, just like I just heard that horrible news and it takes my breath away and I want to scream to wake up from this dream.

General Hondo Campbell sent us an e-mail a few years ago on Gold Star Mother's Sunday and in it he shared the verse below. I go to that verse often for comfort. Even though I can't comprehend the mind of God I am comforted because I know that one day when I get to heaven Josh will come running up to me and once again grab me and hug me with those strong arms of his and welcome me home.

"Good people pass away; the godly often die before their time. But no one seems to care or wonder why. No one seems to understand that God is protecting them from the evil to come. For those who follow godly paths will rest in peace when they die," Isaiah 57:1 NIV

Tired Heart
By Bleach
From the album *"Astronomy"*

I haven't felt good in months
the well has run dry, all at once
the habits come easy, but they're so hard to break
I really need to hear, to hear you say

Peace be still
I am with you
rest in me for one more night
peace be still
I am with you
replace your tired heart with mine

So I'll sing songs of life
for all these broken hearts
just like mine
And I'll lay down
all this pride
so I can hear you whisper
that it's all right

Peace be still
I am with you
rest in me for one more night
peace be still
I am with you
replace your tired heart with mine

And I'm so sorry
I haven't come home
But I'm coming home soon

Story behind the writing of Tired Heart

In May of 2003 Bleach was in the studio recording their album, Astronomy. Lloyd and I had come home for a meeting in Atlanta with the North American Mission Board and I was staying 2 weeks longer than

Lloyd. Lloyd had already returned to Guam so Ashley and I went over to observe and just hang out with the guys several days while they were in the studio working. On one of those occasions we watched as the guys tracked the music for a song that Milam had written called Tired Heart. That night he came home to their apartment where I was already asleep and woke me about 1:30 a.m. (Musician's are nocturnal you know). Upon waking I could tell that he was troubled by something. He began to tell me how it was bothering him that he hadn't had a chance to finish his lyrics to the song that he had written for Josh. A few days prior, Kim had called Milam and Jared and asked them to pray for Josh because he was having a hard time dealing with the trials of war. She had asked them not to share this with us so as Milam told me this, he just said that he felt like Josh may be struggling and felt led to write this song for him. But, he was afraid he would not be able to complete it before they needed to track the vocals. After returning to the studio the next day, Milam explained to Davy (Bleach's singer) the inspiration for the song and how he wanted to write it for Josh. A few short days later and Tired Heart was born. The whole album seemed to be leaning much more somber than Bleach usually did and even they were wondering what exactly that could mean. It was much more contemplative than their usual stuff. They completed the recording and the final product was in the hands of the label. The final mix was sent to the Bleach guys on the day before Josh was killed (July 22) for their approval to release the recording. As we drove back to Nashville from Atlanta that day, July 23, late at night, Milam said he had something for Lloyd and I to listen to. He put the CD in and played Tired Heart. He said, "Mom, this is the song I talked to you about that night after I got back from the studio. I wrote it for Josh." The words were almost haunting. Little did any of us know that Josh would be killed before that song was released. I know that God knew these things and that is why the lyrics were so pressing for Milam that night. The entire album has become a place of solace for our family – one of many pictures of God's sovereignty. All of the songs somehow connect with sadness. God was at work in those guys as they wrote the songs and Astronomy has ministered to us and to others since it came out worldwide in October of 2003.

Two of the members of Bleach came to Fort Carson and sang Tired Heart at the memorial service on July 30. The recording was played at the funeral in South Carolina.

"Without heroes, we are all plain people, and don't know
how far we can go."
-Bernard Malamud

CHAPTER NINE

JOSH'S LAST WORDS

"So my spirit grows faint within me; my heart within
me is dismayed." -Psalm 143:4 NIV

Memorial Day of 2006, was a beautiful spring day, the sun glistened brightly, the birds were chirping in harmony and the wind blew lightly with a refreshing breeze that made one truly appreciate God's handiwork. The army had contacted us a few weeks earlier to invite us to a special ceremony for the purpose of dedicating a memorial to the soldiers from Josh's division who had been killed since Operation Iraqi Freedom began in March 2003.

We were picked up at our motel by the Army's special escort team assigned to us, Captain Andy Watson (the soldier put in charge of the mission to find Josh's killer and his accomplices) and Sergeant Herrera (one of Josh's soldiers who trained and served under him and loved Josh dearly). They were to take care of us the three days we were there. The monument had been designed by the same artist who created the World War II Memorial in Washington, D.C.

We were driven first to the chapel for a religious service in memory of all the fallen. It brought back some bad memories but also some of the wonderful moments we had spent with Josh. One of our visits he and Kim had taken us to this chapel for Sunday services. The first Memorial Service was held for Josh, in this chapel, exactly one week after he had died. There had been only a handful of deaths from Fort Carson then and Josh was number 300 of total military deaths for our nation at this point in the war. As I write this there have been over 4,000 deaths. The chapel was packed with soldiers and their families with some people having to stand outside. The Chaplain shared that he had never seen the chapel this full.

The special service was well organized and it was a beautiful tribute and remembrance of our loved ones. My heart ached for our two escorts as they shed tears over losing Josh and other comrades. It was a learning time for me as I had never really considered how much grief our soldiers endure. A soldier's main objective is to return from every mission with his or her buddy by their side. When a fellow soldier is killed it leaves a lasting imprint on a soldier's life that is unexplainable. I have discovered the main emotion they endure is the guilt. Why did I come back alive and he/she didn't?

After the service we were driven to the memorial site for the dedication. It was beautiful to witness the complete squadron as they lined up in formation as straight as an arrow.

Many of the soldiers and their families spoke to us and shared how much they thought of our son and the relationship they shared. I will always remember one young man in civilian clothes who had just gotten out of the army. He came up to us and was visibly moved. Everyone else who knew Josh had either attended West Point or a special training school with him, or knew him while he served as aide de camp to the general the year before he left for Iraq. This young man shared that he never really knew Josh, but that Josh had a great impact on his life as they were entering Iraq. As their regiment was crossing the border into Iraq from Kuwait he was sorely depressed. He, also a Captain at the time, said that he felt like he couldn't keep going being so homesick and afraid of what they would face. He met a smiling Josh during some of their down time, and asked him why he didn't seem worried, concerned, or afraid. How was he smiling? Josh explained he was all three, "but we have a job to do and our country and our families are depending on us. I have accepted what we need to do, might as well smile, but to tell you the truth I want to go home more than you'll ever know and we will when our mission is over here." This young man even had his journal where he had written what Josh said to him and as he read what Josh said he told us, "Josh's attitude made the difference in how I led my men from then on. I will never forget Josh's smile."

We recently got a copy of Todd's entry that day into his journal and want to include his exact words as recorded in the journal:

"I met Josh Byers today. He was in pretty good spirits for having been screwed over three times in the last 2 years. He gave me a small gem of wisdom

from his father. 'Your attitude is the one thing you have full control over and if it's not positive it's only your fault.' I may have to take that to heart over the next year or so…"

After attending the dedication, we were driven to the Colonel's briefing, the regiment had just recently returned from their second deployment to Iraq. The colonel told us how much he loved and respected Josh and said he would have made general. He told us about a soldier under Josh's command who wanted to talk to us privately. In fact, he was the Humvee driver on the fateful day that Josh was taken from us.

We sat down in the office with Sergeant Tim Buskell and Sergeant Herrera standing behind him. Sergeant Buskell was timid and squirming in his chair, nervous as a cat in a room full of rocking chairs. He shared in detail about the morning Josh died. They were first in the convoy that was moving to set up a new camp in Al Fallujah. Sergeant Buskell was the driver, Josh was in the front passenger seat and the scout, Sergeant Dean Lockhart, manned the machine gun in the center lookout position. He explained that the force of the explosion blew him completely out of the Humvee but luckily he was holding onto the steering wheel tightly. He told us, "My body went out and came back in almost simultaneously." He immediately wanted to slam on the brakes (which is the natural thing to do), but in the midst of the blood and smoke (Sergeant Lockhart was severely injured and Josh's interpreter was gravely injured) he heard Captain Byers in a gravely voice say, "Sergeant, we've hit an IED. Keep moving forward." It was then that Sergeant Buskell hit the gas and moved forward a few yards until the disabled vehicle came to a stop. Sergeant Herrera spoke up at this point and said that by moving forward at least 2 other lives were saved. Sergeant Buskell said as the smoke cleared, Captain Byers looked as though he was in a peaceful sleep as the medic declared him dead.

We left that meeting with our minds numb. It was quite a while before we spoke to one another in our motel room hashing over the very last words of our son. Days turned into weeks with a strange feeling that his words meant something to us. Not only was our son a hero who saved lives, but also he was telling us all something we so desperately need as we face the everyday demons that haunt us.

That is what heroes do…

I had faithfully prayed every day for Josh. After all, I was a missionary assigned to a far away island (over 9,000 miles away) supervising and mentoring young pastors, trying to teach those who were natives to be indigenous and become ministry leaders in their native land. I had been a pastor for 15 years prior to beginning mission work with the beautiful privilege of baptizing several hundred people who had given their lives to Christ. After our pastoral days, where I had joined many couples in matrimony, led our first church in building a parsonage, new worship center and educational space, administered the last rites in over a hundred funeral services, we changed our course and became church planters. What a blessing to have the opportunity and privilege of starting several churches from scratch, not because of a church split but a gathering of those who had not been "churched" (or inoculated with religion) and watching them grow in their spiritual lives. Our first church start was in Sparks, Nevada (just outside Reno), and we were located among over 50,000 people with no other evangelical church in the area at that time.

When we first heard of Josh's death, I guess I was too comfortable as an "experienced minister." The many valleys and mountains we had encountered during those years were a fertile soil for individual spiritual growth. I discovered in July of 2003 that I had become way too comfortable as a Christian and a minister. I had seen it all, or so I thought, in counseling many who had numerous problems. In advising many churches of the next step in representing God in their area of outreach. Again, I thought I had seen and heard it all.

When we left the Atlanta airport that Wednesday afternoon, I was numb and somewhere far away, my emotions nonexistent and feeling as though I wasn't really present. Back at the hotel we tried to calm ourselves and make the necessary phone calls. I remember leaving the others and going across the parking lot. I sat on the curb under the blazing hot Georgia sun as it beat on the asphalt around me. I remember talking to God, "God, I just don't understand." (We do not know the ways of our Lord for there are things that God knows that we do not need to know). He knows the future, and though I believe Josh was taken prematurely, God knew it and has shown His power even in the tragedy. "I prayed to you every day and my faithful prayer was; Please God, protect Josh today." I sat on that hot curb at first numb, not knowing what to do and suddenly blurted out in anger, "But you didn't protect him. Why God, why did you take my boy? Why did you let that happen? I don't understand."

We continued to grieve and cry as we traveled on to Nashville later that night to make plans to fly out to Fort Carson, Colorado, as soon as we could. During the season of memorial services, news interviews, and the funeral, I stumbled through daily life not speaking to God. After two and a half weeks when the formal services were over, we were blessed to stay at a friend's lake house near Chattanooga, Tennessee. We had been given the lake house for as long as we needed. Our sons had given up their apartment just a few weeks before Josh's death to move into a house in August and had been traveling on tour most of July. They had arranged to stay with friends in their small apartment and sleep on the sofa. I will never forget the hospitality of Amanda and Ashley for letting us stay at their apartment many nights during this horrible time we were muddling through. It was truly a blessing to be in such a beautiful, peaceful, and restful setting at the Chattanooga lake house. Some friends came to spend a couple of days with us and truly ministered to us. I tried to hide my spiritual anger, but it was useless. My dear friend, Robert, saw right through me. We can sometimes fool people, never God, but good friends know you inside and out. Robert had been my associate pastor at the church we started in Georgia. He asked me what my problem was with God. I couldn't "pull his leg" so I shared my heart as I wept. He reached out with a heart of love, talked to me straight about what I was doing and God grabbed hold of my heart. Robert explained to me that God may not have protected Josh exactly the way I asked but he did protect him. Josh received his reward much sooner and now doesn't have to deal with this sinful world. When God speaks to your heart it communicates better than if He called you on the phone. I realized He loved me and was taking care of our disaster by revealing the blessing. War is devastating, but God reached down and made something tragic fit together like a puzzle in the perspective of life.

The red light is flashing "trouble" when a person thinks he or she has the patent on spiritual life. My advice to the reader is to check your spiritual life, don't become too "experienced". Many professing Christians have the 'talk' but not the 'walk' and like me, get too comfortable.

I could elaborate on the theological aspect of what happened to me personally with God, and I just speculate that as you read this you have also dealt with "similar" anger or will in the future. My purpose for this book is not one of eschatological theology but the legacy of my son, who is a hero… I would like to leave with you the message of Josh's last words. You may forget everything I've shared but please remember three words; "Keep Moving Forward." That's what heroes do…

"An American officer, intelligent, refined, brave, accomplished in his profession, and with all this a faithful soldier and servant of Christ, is one of those specimens of our nature which we cannot behold without admiration, nor mention without praise."
-Rev. J. W. French, 1857

CHAPTER 10

"A FEW WORDS FROM JOSH"

"I can do all things through Christ who strengthens
me."-Philippians 4:13 NKJV

Josh loved writing since early high school. He would share some of his
poems and short pieces with Mary and me, and we were blown away by
his ability. He may have gotten my looks but he got all of his intelligence
from his mother. I never had Josh's desire to sit down and put my soul
on paper. I know this may sound like bragging, (I am a little prejudiced)
but our three boys are brilliant. I can honestly and sincerely say that. We
tried to create a loving environment in our family and instill in each of
our boys to make the most of what they'd been given. My family is proof
that, if you raise your children by the Word of God and let them know
how loved and special they are, you will be amazed by the integrity that
shines through your children. *The New York Times* printed a few of Josh's
letters on Veteran's Day 2003 and I have included those as well as several
of his poems in this chapter.

A SHORT PRAYER FOR MY FAMILY
By J.T. Byers
November 27, 1994
All the riches in the world and all the power that could ever be laid at my
feet could never compare to the overwhelming blessing that my family is
to me. Thank you, O Lord, for my loved ones. Help us all to bring pride to
our name and favor from you onto our entity as a family as we seek to do
your will in our lives. Our personalities, our strength and weaknesses, our

purposes, are all strikingly different. But when brought together in love, in your service, our uniqueness produces a beautiful melody to your ears just as a sweet sounding orchestra consists of many different instruments. We have had our share of hard times, and will continue to have them I am willing to bet. But help us to always lean on You and each other in the midst of our trials so that we may grow even stronger as a result of these confrontations with our weaknesses. May we never take each other for granted, and be there when our loved ones need us. In your mighty and loving hand we commend our family – a testimony to your grace, power, and love. Amen.

DARE TO DREAM
By Cadet Joshua T. Byers, USMA 1996

It began as a little boy's prayer
A dream conjured from destiny
And wrapped in swaddling innocence
Seeds of direction planted by the will of God
Watered by His grace
Cared for by His love.

Time marched as the long line stretched
Nearer and nearer to my yearning soul
Apparitions of the past's glory
Paraded tauntingly in my sleep
Ghost of the gray
Lifeblood of liberty.

Achievement rang with the echo of sacrifice
The appointment given with accolades and praise
Life's most treacherous valley behind its mountaintops
Indescribable pain wrapped in a dream.

Teary goodbye's marked its beginning
Tearful prayers manifest in its continuation
The desire to win, diluted by the craving to quit.
The hand of God holding my every worry

His tender love gripping deliverance – in His time.

Throughout the year, joy was sparsely woven
Between the entangled sacrifices that were the weeks.
Homecoming comes and speedily goes
Giving way to the slowing tread of time
Days take on the illusion of eternity
The tempo slowed to a deliberate beat.

Daily, fear awakened me from my peaceful sleep
Staring defiantly into my confused and bloodshot eyes.
Slowly, meeting its death
Beaten by new growth in Christ.
Slaughtered by faith in His unfailing love.

I stand, hand held high, gripping Heaven's outstretched hands
The goal closer than ever before
Plebe year will end in a culmination of the power of love
The love of God, and my family
The prayers of a virtuous woman, a steadfast man, and committed brothers
Prayers of men and women of God whom I have never met.

Keeping my bloodied chin up in the midst of toil and strife
Nothing more than a crude instrument in God's unfailing plan
My life traveling the road not taken
Embodied by the simple prayer of a little boy with a dream.

(UNNAMED POEM)
J.T. Byers
24 Dec 94

I am no one special, save through your grace
And yet, the blessings befallen upon me
Are far too numerous to count and
Scores more plentiful than I ever deserve

I have committed my life to your service
In whatever capacity your will leads me to fulfill.
And yet, my sinful nature ne'er fails to surface.

I, alone, have nothing to offer except my very being
And that is yours, Lord, my all.
I shamefully lay my inadequacies at your nail-scarred feet
As you lovingly toss them away, filling me with your Spirit.

Through my weaknesses, those shortcomings, you are strong
Though I feel I have nothing to offer,
You feel differently – you use me as your vessel
You fill me to overflow with your love, grace, and power.

So many others seem to be so much worthier servants than I.
I hardly feel worthy to be your representative on earth
And I am not…alone – As your Holy Spirit dwells within me,
The same spirit that gave the disciples the power to work
miracles in your name. The same spirit you called upon in your
time on this earth.

I am open, and that is enough. I am willing to make whatever
Sacrifice is needed for the kingdom, and that is all you have asked.
For you came to a stable in Bethlehem to do your work,
You went to fishermen to be your disciples to assist in that work,
And you have come to me, in my heart, to continue that same work.

You believed in me 2,000 years ago when my existence could not have
been fathomed,
and I believe in you and the power that you hold inside of me today, as I
move forward in that power, taking heaven by storm, fighting the good
fight in your Name – past my inadequacies, in rebellion of the mortal
hindrances that may seem to control me, forward in your redeeming
power, cleansed by the blood—my inadequacies washed away.

You have overcome the world and all that is in it
So I will not fear, your cross I will bear.
Please lay it upon my shoulders.

STAND
(Being a Christian Soldier)
Joshua T. Byers
January 1994

Duty is mine, events are God's
Adamantly into every fear, into every threat, into every dream.
I ride the horse of truth and carry the weapon of character,
Faith in God has set me above the ensnaring fear of man.
The world is adverse to me; I am a stranger, an outlaw
To some I am destruction, to others I am a haven.

All who are noble and worthy, trustworthy and true
Stand behind me in the storm, I will not fail you.
In the fell clutch of circumstance, I take my stand;
I'll take the chance, I'll run the extra mile.
To take a stand is to be lonely, lonely I will be;
Under the smoking gun of my enemies, I charge.
There is no greater strength than that which is in me.

The power of the Father, the power of love;
Backbone of steel, heart soft as down,
I am willing to make the sacrifice for the higher crown.
His will is all that matters, His purpose is mine,
In the good times and in the bad, He is with me.
Forever I will serve Him, as he guides me through the night;
Never, never will I quit.

"…the kingdom of heaven suffers violence,
and violent men take it by force."
Matthew 11:12

LOVE'S IMPACT
Joshua T. Byers
20 Feb 1994

My life is a race, with what I do not know
With time perhaps, in that struggle to grow
As I stroll through my past in memory's embrace
I can find but one thing constant in that inconsistent race
When times were at their worst, and the sun refused to shine
It was love that kept me nourished and got me out of the bind

When the cards were stacked against me and all hope was lost,
It was love that picked me up and dusted me off
When life seemed a void and loneliness crept in
The odds were against me and I could find no friend
It is there that I found it, pushing me on
Giving me the courage and strength to drive on
It was there in my family through the good and the bad
Never letting me give up, but still loving me if I had

Praise the Lord for our sufferings and times filled with doubt
For it is then that we see that His love will never run out
And this I know – tough times never last, but tough people do
And it is love that sustains them till life's race is through.

MY SOLDIERS
U.S. Military Academy, Class of 1996
25 January 1995

I am accountable, I am responsible,
I am charged with your life.
My decisions dictate your direction
In rank, I stand above you
In service, I fight with you, for you

In the hour of decision,
In the moment of chaos,
In the flash of flying shrapnel,

Our mission stands before us.
Across the torrential river of blood and sacrifice that is battle
I stand, bloodied but unbowed, as your bridge across it.

You serve the great nation we call home.
You protect the birthright of every American,
Save criticism and spittle from the people you serve.
The American soldier – the legacy of commitment,
The history of sacrifice, the blood of freedom—
Stands between our country and those who would harm it
Between peace and chaos
Between life and death
Adamantly proclaiming, "I will protect you with my life"

And I, I stand before you,
You great and noble warriors of freedom,
And proclaim, "Follow me, I will lead you to victory."
With the sons and daughters of America entrusted to my care
I charge under the smoking guns of the enemy
Fighting, killing, laying all of me aside
For my soldiers.

The following letters from Josh to us were written when he first arrived in Iraq from Kuwait to the Monday before that fateful Wednesday morning when Josh was taken from this world. Mary and I truly love our boys and they love us. God gives us our children to raise and teach through actions not words, what honor, integrity, honesty and commitment are. We do not own them, we are just caring for what God so graciously gives us. Our family shares these letters with you. My tears continue to fall even as I type. I miss you, Josh and love you with all my heart, I look forward to being all together again, in Heaven.

Saturday 26 April 03
0643 Zulu

Dear Mom and Dad,

Well, Here I am in Iraq. We left Kuwait 3 days ago and crossed the border. Now we're about 30 miles south of Baghdad. We're getting ready to head west in the next day or so and will be hunting for bad guys in all the areas where American troops haven't been yet. The conditions here are tough, we've been driving pretty hard and you can't ever really totally relax because you never know where the bad guys are. Everybody's fine so far, though, everything's going pretty well. The Iraqi people that we've seen so far (all of southern Iraq up to here) are terribly poor – bad living conditions. Definitely third-world living conditions. When we roll through a town, hundreds of people line the streets and wave Iraqi money at us. They try to reach everything they can grab off of our vehicles and us. Most are happy to see us, it seems. They think that a lot of them are waving their money to pay us for their freedom – it is their culture to give things in return for things given to them. I've told all my guys not to take any of it –for one, I don't want to stop moving and two, I'm sure that these people are waving all the money they have in the world at us. The children are so cute – especially the little girls. They wave and smile – you'd think we were Santa Claus in a Christmas parade!

In every town, you can see the women working the fields, in their traditional black dress and veil. They seem to do most all of the work – I'm not sure what the men do. The only ones working in the fields, that we've seen, were on tractors – I don't think they allow women to operate machinery here. I do have something to tell Dad – We were around a pile of rubble that someone probably lived in and out came a bright green John Deere tractor with about 4 dudes piled on top of it! Even here, all the men want to do is ride a John Deere! I took a picture for you, Dad, I hope it turns out.

I'd better get back to work out here – my down time is over. I'll keep writing you whenever I get the time to put pen to paper! I love you both very much and miss you terribly. I think about you countless times a day and pray for you every time I think of you. I hope everything's going well for you. I love you very much!!!

Love, JT

28 June 03
Ar Ramadi, Iraq

Dear Mom and Dad,
I found a few minutes here to write – Yee haw! I've been in command for 2 weeks now and it has been non-stop. I love command, though. Commanding soldiers is what everything I've done since 1992 has been preparing me for—it is an honor and privilege to lead these men, especially in these times and in this place. I am entirely focused on accomplishing our mission and bringing everyone home safe and sound from here out. There are so many things I can't control, that none of us can control, but we will make sure firmly that we master everything we can affect. I don't really believe in luck, and if I do, I firmly believe that we make our own luck in life. I am always thinking about what more we can do to bring this situation under control and protect American soldiers at the same time. The Colonel has a lot of faith in me and Fox Troop, as evidenced by the degree to which he allows me to exercise complete authority in my assigned area and mission. We are moving back to the Habbaniyah & Fallujah area soon and may have already been there a few days by the time you receive this letter, I'm sure. Our time in AR Ramadi for the past month was very successful. We attacked very aggressively and rewarded compliance with aid money and clothes/school supplies/sports equipment for kids in neighborhoods that didn't shoot at us.

Fallujah is still the hot spot of the country, it seems, as we go back in there...Fox Troop has been assigned responsibility for the majority of the city; I'll also have an MP (military police) platoon attached to me to help. I'm just now starting to think about how we'll go about our talks there. Whatever course of action I decide, it will be very aggressive. I'm convinced that the more violent we are at the start, the less they will want to test us, or fight us. We'll see..........You have to take the "Old West" Tombstone approach, I think. "You tell 'em, I'm coming! And hell is coming with me!"

I can tell already that it will be tough for all of us to transition back to life in the states after this is over. However, it is not all fighting here, we do show much compassion, to the kids mostly, at the same time—it's awesome. We conducted a raid of an Islamic extremist's house that had been coordinating attacks against us, a few days ago. We surrounded the house and had a little firefight inside to nab the guy. None of us were shot, but 3 of the men in the house were (they shot at us first). We pulled them out; I stood at the front door talking on the radio to all involved and higher. I was wrapped up in the situation, getting the house under control and making sure we weren't taking fire from anywhere else—I looked across the lawn and saw one of my soldiers calming down a little girl (probably 2 or 3 years old) –cute as a button and crying her head off—as you can imagine. We get one candy a week (on average) –not counting what we may get from care packages. He was giving her his candy bar, feeding it to her a piece at a time until she stopped crying. He did that just moments after being shot at and shooting men in this girl's house, probably her Dad or brother/ cousin. It really touched me – we have so much heart—as an Army, as a country – compared to the rest of the world. Even as this soldier's uniform bore the blood smears of those he had to shoot for trying to harm us, he showed much compassion to that little girl. I walked over and picked up the little girl, told the soldier to help search the house for more weapons, and thanked him for taking care of her. I gave her to her mother and we wrapped things up and left the area. I love the American soldier – he is someone to be revered by all Americans.

Basically though, we're just taking this all one day at a time. Supposedly, they're going to start building up our base camp in Fallujah. Installing windows and doors on the buildings, even having air conditioning, a mess hall, and even a dayroom with a TV. We have no idea when we'll be able to come home – it's hard not knowing and we're all so incredibly homesick.

I miss you both like crazy! Thank you so much for your letters and most of all your prayers. I love you!!! I can't wait to see you again soon! "Tell Guam I'm coming! And Kimbo's comin' with me! Ha!

I love you!

Love,
JT

18 July 03

Dear Mom and Dad,
Greetings from the Iraqi desert! I'm sitting in my Humvee trying to endure the heat of the afternoon… We generally try to conduct operations in the morning, evening and during the night and stay as inactive as possible during the hottest times of the day. We topped 120 degrees today already and it's only about 1400 hours (2 o'clock PM).

I hope and trust that everything is going well in Guam. You know what I'm talking about when it comes to heat, I'm sure. My letters from you seem to be upbeat – I get the impression that you both see a great need there and feel your call for that place stronger than ever. I can't wait to visit you there! I look forward to meeting all of the people you've told me about in letters. Not to mention getting to learn to Scuba dive!

Life here continues to be challenging, but we're all hanging in there. We got a blow to our morale a few days ago when the Corps Commander visited us (3 Star General). He said there was no way we were going home in less than 9 – 12 months. Man, that's going to suck. We're working on month #4 right now and it already seems like we've been here forever and a day.

I still love being a commander. I love leading troops & taking care of them. It is a huge responsibility and I feel the weight of it every day. I send the thing I love most out here – my men –into harm's way every day and every night. I just do my best to ensure they're ready, trained, equipped & properly lead in every situation. Commanding a Cavalry Troop in combat is very special for that reason. Commanding in combat period has to be one of the most completely demanding things I can think of. That said, it is amazing how well the Army has prepared me for this since I entered West Point. I can even understand the point to a lot of the stuff they made me do plebe year! Ha!

We've been out of the city for the past few days – to be honest, it's been really nice. We came out to the desert north of AR Ramadi to search for & clear enemy base camps/terrorist camps & weapons/ammo storage sites. We got intel that the bad guys were hiding out in the desert, or at least hiding their weapons & ammo there, & coming into the cities to attack us & innocent civilians. The mission has been very successful. We've found a lot of ammunition out here – including a lot of RPGs & Mortar Rounds which are the enemy's weapons of choice. It feels good to be on the offensive & not just waiting to be shot at before we can take bad guys & their "tools" off the street. We're going in tonight & will hit the city again full force tomorrow. The stress never ends here.

Just before coming out to the desert I ate dinner with a Sheik (religion/political leader). He was trying to convince me to let one of his tribesmen out of jail. His "boy" shot at my 3rd platoon with an RPG. He's very lucky to have lived through 3rd platoon's response. I'm not letting the bastard go. The food was O.K. – lamb, chicken, rice and a bread that's pita-like (very good bread). They eat with their hands – all from the same plate (which is huge). Pretty gross!

I think one of the different things about this war when compared to others is that as a combat commander, I also assume the role of Sheriff & Mayor in addition to military commander. During part of a day, I may be meeting with city elders/leaders about issues within the city. A few hours later, my men & I are kicking in doors & exchanging gunfire with "anti-coalition factions" or people who have committed grievous criminal acts. Very interesting, I guess.

I really miss home though! I miss Kim with all my heart and can tell that she is having a really hard time with this even though she does a good job of showing me she's being strong.

I love you both very much & miss you like crazy! I can't wait to see you & pray every day that it will be soon! I love you!!!

Love,
JT

The following letter is the very last letter Josh wrote to us. He wrote it two days before his death. Two months after Josh's funeral and memorial services, we returned to Guam. We made our usual trip to the Post Office and this letter was there. Needless to say, it was a very emotional time.

21 JUL 03
AR Ramadi,
IRAQ

Dear Mom & Dad,
Hey! I'm doing well – healthy and safe so far in Iraq about 4 months. I received another package from you yesterday along with a letter from Dad. You go above & beyond for me, your support is amazing – I am so thankful for you! You don't need to send so much – but everything you send gets used by me or a soldier that needs it more than me.

Dad's letter was so great to read – it was typed so it looks like you're getting used to the computer, Dad! The letters from both of you are so comforting – it feels so great to come in dirty & sweaty from a mission to a letter, or letters sometime, lying on my cot. I hope Kim & I can one day be half the parents you are.

It sounds like Guam is awesome from your letters. Sounds like the need there is so great & that you are fulfilling a great need there for the missionaries, pastors & laypeople on the islands. I loved reading what you wrote about the young Chinese girls that work in the factories in Saipan and their love for Christ. I can't wait to come & see you in Guam and meet as many of these people as possible!

We conducted a huge operation in the desert about a week ago. We had intel that suggested that the bad guys were hiding weapons & ammo out in the desert & bringing it into the city to attack us. We swept all of the desert north of AR Ramadi & found lots of weapons/ammo. Very successful! Just yesterday (2 days after coming in from the desert), we conducted a raid on some leaders/members of a group called the Noor Mohammed Group. Bad dudes – smuggling arms from Syria & conducting attacks on US troops. We captured all of the targets we were after & lots of weapons. 2 of the targets that we captured (Fox Troop) turned out to be 1st cousins of Saddam Hussein, we found all kinds of "Saddam stuff in their house". We have good intel that Saddam has hidden in this house over the past 2 months...Wouldn't it be great if we caught the big fish! Wow! It's possible! I think I'd probably get my chance to be on Jay Leno if that happened! 'Ya think?' Ha!

I can't wait to hear Bleach's new album. I miss Milam and Jared very much. I can't wait until the next time the whole family is together!

I love you both with all of my heart! I'm working very hard here – adding honor to our country and to our family! As they say in Georgia, "I ain't skeered!" We're fighting our way home! I love you both!

I miss you!

Love,
JT

"Winning isn't everything—but wanting to win is."
-Vince Lombardi

CHAPTER ELEVEN

MOVING FORWARD AS WE PERSEVERE

"I praise you because I am fearfully and wonderfully made; your works are wonderful, I know that full well."
Psalm 139:14 NIV

I discovered some time ago that this life really doesn't have much to offer us. As pastor of one of our church plants several years ago, I met a middle-aged man who had everything one could ask for materially. He lived in a beautiful home with furnishings that you were almost afraid to touch. He drove luxury cars and played golf at his fancy country club. He asked me to lunch one day, and told me of his success over the years. As I got to know him better, I found myself feeling really sorry for him; his life was just one business deal after another. He never seemed at ease because it was never enough. He didn't talk about how great it was to love and give love to his family and friends. When I challenged him about being too busy for family time he mumbled that they would have to understand, there is money out there to be made. He tried his best to portray an intelligent, brilliant achiever in how to get rich. He was smart and successful in the business world, but he just didn't get it. Life is a series of ups and downs and if we focus on the wrong thing, it is like getting on a merry-go-round, then getting off at the same place where you got on. We haven't made any progress in real life but have managed to convince ourselves that we are really moving.

The more I contemplated those last words of a dying soldier, the more I began to "get it." We desperately need to move forward in the pursuit of life's meaningful challenges. In this true story of our son, the immediate reaction to keep moving forward actually saved two other lives. It is in this very similar battle that we find ourselves. No matter what circumstances of life you find yourself in, consider the lives involved and affected by your decisions, including your own.

Our immediate reaction is to slam on the brakes when something critical happens – a child's sickness, marital problems, bad news from the doctor, overdrawn funds with no hope of help, the death of someone you loved more than life – we just have the tremendous urge to slam on the brakes of who we are as individuals. We get trapped in a corner emotionally feeling like there is nowhere to turn. Life seems too difficult to face and I can't do it anymore. There are critical issues that lie ahead, people's lives are hanging in the balance (including our own), and we just want to slam on the brakes with our emotions and shut completely down hoping it will all just go away.

We've got to "keep moving forward" even though that involves making some tough decisions because the consequences are a matter of life and death. If we have God's love in our lives, our willingness to "move forward" may be an instrument of God to save the one who is by our side. We can't stop moving, shutting down the very wheels that will change our life. We must envision the whole picture of the battle as well as the decision to keep on keeping on. If we aren't moving forward we are slipping backward.

Dare to move on. When traffic gets bogged down in our mundane lives we want to stop, go back, and get out of the pressure. Face the storms of life and get back up even when you're knocked down. We are all vulnerable and no one can stand alone in the fiercest of storms, but dare to move on with trust in Christ and rise in the midst of "blood and smoke."

I remember watching a track competition on TV years ago and one of the runners caught my eye, he seemed so determined. His determined spirit seemed to jump out to me from the TV screen. I watched intently and was fascinated by his desire to win. As he came around the last curve to the finish line, ahead by several feet I found myself cheering like a die-hard fan (I didn't even know his name or team) but he stood out as a winner. Suddenly he began to show signs of struggle, slowing down while others passed him as they neared the finish line. He then tripped and fell face first against the cinder running track. I thought, "Oh well, you win some and lose some." I was blown away by what happened next. He laid there motionless, not moving a muscle, then out of nowhere, lifted himself up and began crawling to the finish line which was still about a hundred yards away. I stood in front of that television and cheered him on. I was moved so in my spirit I began to cry. With every move on his hands and knees I cried and cheered for this hero. He was determined to keep moving forward. As he slowly moved, you could see the blood running down his wrists and arms. His knees were so soaked in blood it looked as though he was wearing bright red kneepads. He kept moving forward, and I stood there with tears; emotionally drained yet totally revived as if I had taken a cold shower. What a winning spirit. He would not quit nor let anyone help him. He was determined to reach the finish line. I cried and cheered along with the stadium full of spectators. It is interesting that very few people cheered the one who came in first, however, it seemed like the whole world cheered this last place finisher who in reality was the real winner. He was knocked down but not knocked out. He could have put on the brakes and stopped. He had a great excuse to quit, but his choice to keep moving forward made a difference in my life that day. I was totally renewed with a fresh attitude, as I was amidst some really tough situations and decisions at that time.

We have to be willing, no matter the circumstances that we find ourselves in, to push forward with determination that we **can** make life-changing decisions that will make a difference. We must be committed to that life giving sacrifice. Josh may have lost his physical life but he immediately went to be with our Heavenly Father because of Jesus Christ. He made a difference in so many lives and his legacy lives on.

We continue to receive e-mails and letters from soldiers and civilians who have completely changed their lives after hearing of Josh's death. Lives being changed spiritually and moving forward with a life that serves mankind.

You need to "keep moving forward" with the perseverance of not stopping but looking out in a dark world full of man's inhumanity to man to make a difference. We all have a mission to fulfill in life, a purpose, with many waiting to see if we will get back up and dare to move on. "Drive on!" as Josh so often said.

The Bible puts it rather to the point. In Hebrews 12:1 says, "Therefore, since we are surrounded by such a huge crowd of witnesses to the life of faith, let us strip off every weight that slows us down, especially the sin that so easily trips us up. And let us run with endurance the race God has set before us." (NLT)

God did not teach us to always be number one in life's races, but He did tell us to hit the gas, not the brakes, as we face the storms and "keep moving forward."

We have heard it said many times that someone wants to "bear their soul." They want to share the whole of their feelings. When we open up in this way we do feel vulnerable as if we were naked. We have to be willing to face the reality of the kind of world in which we live. We discover everyone is searching, trying to find the meaning to life and the answer to the question of what will happen to their soul, which does NOT die when the body dies. God looks down on us and gives us the greatest opportunities ever, and we take it for granted. God loves you more than there are words to write and He is willing and ready to be there for you, to love you, meet your needs, and accept you as you are. God desires you to love Him for who He is; the God of the Universe. He doesn't expect you to walk around with the family Bible and stop people to witness to. He wants you to teach through action and word, the multitudes of how much God loves them. To understand that, takes faith in believing who Jesus is. We simply seek God's forgiveness for our past, God will hear us and immediately forgive us and reach out with His loving arms to embrace us as His child. When we realize we are a part of God's family, we are free to be and do what God would have us to be and do. It may be to continue doing what you have been doing but with a different attitude that faces life's difficulties with a calm but determined spirit. He may be calling you to something new. Perhaps God is calling you to a specific work in His great plan that no one can accomplish but you. If we could just "get it." God wants to make us free from the old self, free to take risks of faith. When we experience that freedom, we begin to take on that new self as we risk the impossible. Let God move in your life, He will direct you and believe me He will get your attention as to what He wants you to do. It doesn't have to be something that you've seen before. Venture out into unknown territory when God begins speaking to your heart, and you will never be the same again. God loves to take the mundane life and make it exciting. I know some folks can't understand how God would love them as I've described. Jesus used the little children to illustrate to us that we are just like a child. We must come as a child with fresh, enthusiastic trusting faith to Him. Jesus reached out to the thief on the cross who had lived a very sinful and undeserving life. At that moment as Jesus was dying for our sins on the cross, the thief reached out with childlike faith and asked our Lord, "Will you remember me when you come into your Kingdom?" Jesus said, "Yes, TODAY you will enter into Paradise." He realized who God was and simply asked his Lord to "accept him and forgive his sins."

Our precious Word of God never changes. I believe it is the inerrant word of God and has no mistakes. However, we as a culture change. I'm glad we don't have "outhouses" anymore, and we can go to our own private bathrooms inside our homes. I'm so happy we don't have to haul wood inside our homes anymore for the woodstove. It is a plain miracle that we can push a button on the thermostat and have heat or cold air. As I look at the church today, there is no urgency in our fellow Christian's attitude. Maybe God wants us to change gears to make something happen. We have to keep moving forward to advance the kingdom of God, and I don't see many churches doing whatever it takes, total change, if necessary to reach with the loving, soul- saving message of Christ. As the commercial says, "Just do it!" Dare to step out and witness God's amazing power. It is my prayer that you will allow God to do something even as you read this, something unique and special. My heart beats to see the unchurched claimed for Christ. My prayer is that we reach out with a Godly non-judging love. Be willing to share about the God who changes lives and who gives hope in a world full of hate, war, and death.

I could not keep on keeping on without hope. My hope is in Christ who will one day open up to us the gates of Heaven. A place with streets of gold and mansions without sin, tears, or pain. Where we will see our Lord Jesus Christ, and our loved ones who have gone on before us. Heaven is forever. I read that just the beginning of eternity is like when a small sparrow takes one grain of sand in its beak on our east coast and flies to the west coast to deposit it. When that bird completely takes all the sand from the entire east coast, it is just the beginning of Heaven. My first question to Josh when I see that wide grin of his and he picks me up for a hug is, "Have you had any sweet tea?"

"It matters not if the world has heard or approves or understands. The only applause I am meant to seek is that of nail-scarred hands."
2 Lieutenant Joshua T. Byers, June 1, 1996
(West Point Graduation)

CHAPTER TWELVE

HOW TO HELP THE GRIEVING

"Precious in the sight of the Lord is the death of His
Saints."
Psalm 116:15 NIV

I have always said of my doctorate degree (Doctor of Ministry) that God doesn't really need doctors because He is not sick, and never will be. However, it is just a D.Min. not a medical doctorate, and merely the result of wanting to further my education in ministry. I really liked the title when I first graduated with colors, it went to my head. I guess that was a mark of my immaturity at the time, but now I am almost embarrassed when someone introduces me as "Dr. Byers." I am really not as smart as it implies. Josh was in sixth grade when I received my doctoral degree (I squeezed a 4 year bachelor's degree into 10 years), Milam was in third grade and Jared was a whopping three years old. They all sat in the auditorium along with their mother and watched me "walk the aisle." Josh went to school the following week and told one of his teachers that his dad was now a doctor. She asked him what was my specialty and Josh answered, "Oh, he is not the kind of doctor that can help you." Wow, speaking of becoming humble when one thinks that he is pretty big. In the following weeks, Josh gave his homeroom teacher a check for his yearbook and the check had "Dr. and Mrs. Lloyd Byers" at the top (another ego thing for me) to which his teacher immediately asked, "Would you ask your dad what kind of pain this may be in the middle of my back and what should I do about it?" Without changing expressions Josh answered that he would ask and let her know. Without saying anything to me until sometime later,

Josh went back to school the next morning and told her, "Dad said it is probably a pulled muscle because you sit at your desk so much, so take two aspirins and rest." She thanked Josh repeatedly for the help. Josh told us the story at the dinner table a few days later, and I don't think I have ever laughed harder! That is probably what most of these kinds of doctorates are good for, a laugh (please, no offense to Dr. Williams, my mentor in post graduate study).

I know nothing about medicine. But I do know that when a person is hurting, whether it is physical or emotional pain, you need to see the expert who is highly trained. I know full well the pious arguments from the fundamental religious side that often remind us, from the pulpit that one does not need medicine for their emotional problems, one just needs to "trust in the Lord." I certainly cannot argue with the fact that we need to trust in the Lord and that faith is the step we take to allow our hearts to be comforted by Him. However, we need to understand that God did allow doctors and research experts to gain the knowledge of medications to help with our struggles and hurts in life. What is important is to take into consideration that the chemicals in our brains can get out of whack just like an infection can take over and make us really sick. When the infection occurs, physicians may prescribe an antibiotic and/or other medications. When we get depressed and don't want to get out of bed, then just as an infection or as critical as breaking a bone, we immediately need medical attention. Why is it wrong then, when our emotional thinking breaks down, to get medical help? I am not talking about a medication that is addicting, but one that helps treat the imbalance of chemicals. There are a lot of alternative ways to treat depression and anxiety and each person is different in their choice of treatment. I believe that God gives us brains and doctors to do what needs to be done for our health and our faith. I don't believe God expects us to suffer if we have a remedy readily available to us. Just as we would put a cast on a broken bone we should do what needs to be done. It is necessary to take care of our emotional sufferings. Mary and I both do not apologize for having taken antidepressants to keep us going and to get us back on track. I want to assure you who grieve that, I believe in reaching out not only by sharing God's love but also to help with the struggles in our minds with medical help. It is not something to be ashamed of. Yes, God is the ultimate eternal solution, but He often uses medicine to get us to that point. I do not believe there is a sinful chasm between medicinal use and faith-based living.

After going through the uneasy funeral services, visitation, memorial services (three in our case) and receiving many visitors, I heard many theological reasons that everything would be alright. Please, don't get me wrong, I appreciated every thoughtful and kind word. I know full well what family and friends were attempting to do by comforting the grieving in such a way. Many think they have "comfort wording" in the bag, and it should just make you want to shout for joy when we hear their thesis on death and what God will do. Having been a pastor for 28 years and participating in many, many funerals, I had never really been on the receiving side. I truly loved many of the ones I had conducted funerals for and some seemed like my own family; therefore, I grieved in a different way as a pastor and as a dad. It becomes a different ballgame when the person in the casket is a member of your family. Mary and I had lost her mother, my father, and Mary's father before we had the burden of burying our own son. We've heard some pretty weird stuff from those who really don't know what to say. However, there is a gigantic difference in burying your parents as opposed to burying your own child. You love your parents, but burying your child is just not the natural order of things. As our parents get older, we know that time will handle that which is inevitable but it is not natural to lose a young son who had such a promising future ahead of him. I do know God has a plan and His ways are not my own, but in my humanness, I questioned Him.

Before it was laid on my heart to write this book I had full intentions of writing a book entitled, "What NOT to say at a funeral." I mentioned this several times when preaching or speaking and became inundated with many who said, "Please write it soon, I want to know." Some well-meaning people really want to attend the funeral of their loved one, but don't simply because they just don't know what to say to the family. We feel a pressure to say something that will fix the hurts, but that is not at all what we need to do. People truly mean well when they try to encourage and comfort the grieving, but you hear some of the most insensitive statements made, of all places, in the funeral home or graveside.

Let me first tackle what to say to a friend, relative, or neighbor who has lost a spouse, child, friend, etc. What are the magic words that will leave them comforted? There are no magic words that will make one feel better at that time. Nothing you can say will take away the pain one is going through from losing the most precious person in their life. The most important thing many did for us as Josh lay in that box was simply their presence. They did not say a thing to justify his death. The most comforting thing is to show your tears, your empathy, that you are grieving alongside me and truly sorry for the loss. That is it in a nutshell. It is simple. To grab and hold them tight and through tear-stained eyes say, "I am sorry." It's a comfort to know someone grieves alongside you. You can't justify the death by, "he or she is better off than we are, you know" but a hug shows that you understand my hurt. The one grieving needs you, not the 1,001 explanations of death you think may comfort them. They are stunned, shocked, and missing their loved one. They don't need to hear how much better his or her death is in the sight of the Lord. (Even though that is true.) All they know in this moment is that there is a void in their life.

These are some of the statements said to us when Josh died. "Well, you have two other children so it is not so bad…" What? Is that like just adding more cows to the herd and everything will be all right? We must truly consider "thinking" through what to say to one who has literally lost their reason to live. God made that marvelous creation who is being laid to rest, there is no other person living who can take their place. It doesn't matter if we have 50 children, not one of them would be Josh. Therefore, do not assume that because we have other boys, that helps with our grief.

On visitation night at the funeral home in Laurens, South Carolina, we visited with hundreds of people and were told so many "comforting" things that it became difficult to hear. We heard about other's death experiences with family and "You'll get over it, I did," "Time heals," etc. We were grieving, because our son was lying in a casket, and that relationship was unique and unlike any other. We heard "Things will get better," "Don't worry, he is with the Lord," "You've got to put this behind you and move on," "Hang in there, everything will be alright," "I know exactly how you feel because I lost an uncle two years ago." I heard so much I wanted to scream. I wanted to shout back, "I will not get over it, can't you see, this is my son, my best friend," or "I know he is with the Lord," "I am so very grateful that I will see him again but I miss him now!" And "No, no, no, you don't know exactly how I feel, this is my son, not my uncle!" One person even said she knew how we felt, because she had recently lost her cat.

Always be mindful of what you can do for the family who has lost their loved one. Many times as you are busy elsewhere doing every day routines; and it occurs to you to do something kind for the grieving family, you need to act now! I've heard countless times from many, "I really meant to bring a meal by, have you over, cut your grass, come and get the kids and take them to the park," etc. Good intentions never accomplish anything. When this occurs to you, God is putting this person or family on your heart. Let them know you are there; be of service to them. Another common mistake is, asking, "Is there anything I can do?" Don't even ask just DO It. DO something. Check into their personal situation and find out the needs. People will call and say, "Call me if you ever need anything." Ninety-nine percent of people will say, "Okay, I will," with absolutely no intention of ever calling you. Go over to their house and let them know you are going to do something. Ask them, and if they do not provide an answer, then you decide what you will do. Mow their lawn, cook a meal, clean the house, buy them a restaurant gift card, babysit, offer to help write thank-you notes, run errands for them, whatever you can think of, just do not forget to help. They will not call you, and even everyday tasks are huge for someone in grief.

Keep dates on your calendar of when tragic events occurred in the lives of your friends and loved ones. When that date rolls around write them a card to say, "I am thinking of you today, and I am so sorry about your great loss a year ago." (2 years, 3 years, etc.) It is important to us that our loved one be remembered. Let them know you are praying for them. What a blessing that is as you care, you love; therefore, they know they are not alone on those difficult days and their loved one is not forgotten.

On the third anniversary of Josh's death, Mary and I were both on staff at a church in Franklin, Tennessee. Two of the church members called Mary at the office the day before the anniversary and said they wanted to bring something by for us. One sweet friend brought two casseroles and trimmings for two meals to have that evening and the next day. She had two preschoolers and had her hands full. How touching for her to take the time to think of us. Another family stopped by to bring a beautiful flower arrangement and a very sweet note about how they had been blessed by seeing our faith through our loss. There were times when we felt like we weren't being a help to anyone, we weren't handling things like we should, but to have someone say those words meant the world to us. It's not just what you say, but what you do and how much it comes from your heart that matters. You can be a blessing!

When we traveled back to Guam after Josh's funeral we had two of the most loving families reach out and minister to us in such a meaningful and beautiful way. They met us at the airport, brought us our car, and took us out to our favorite restaurant. They comforted us as we sat and talked. They were "our family" there, and we would sit and talk for hours into the night many times. As time passed they were always checking on us, and asking us to come over just to hang out; order pizza and watch a movie. They were there for us. That is one of the greatest things you can do in a grief situation, just be there!

I am amazed at the things that have unfolded since we lost our son. Josh made such an impression on his family and friends that he also has the honor of several babies (around 10) being named after him or in memory of him. Even years before his death he had a namesake in Nevada. He shared how that blessed him to have such an honor. Our oldest Grandson, (the Bump) is named: Joshua Gunnar Byers. Uncle Josh would be so proud. There were even two girls named in Josh's memory. One is Liberty, the daughter of our friends on Guam, born one year after Josh's death. Another is, Honor, one of the Bleach member's little girl born toward the end of 2004. A lot of thought went into these names, and we were so touched by their tribute. I can see him smiling now.

Josh bought his first home in Colorado when he was transferred to Fort Carson from Fort Leonard Wood, Missouri. He and Kim bought a house in Fountain, Colorado, near the back gate of Fort Carson. I remember Josh calling to tell us that he found his first house, and he was excited like a child at Christmastime. He insisted on meeting the developer, not just the sales representative, to make sure it was built right as well as trying to talk him down in price. (He said he got that from his dad.) When we arrived at their home a few days after his death, the developer came by to speak to us. After introducing himself, he shared his sadness and hurt. He told us how he had met Josh and said he had never had a customer quite like him, he bragged on his attention to detail. He shared how much he had been touched by the fine, gentleman-like spirit that Josh had. After his condolences, he told us that he had a little business to conduct. When he heard of Josh's death, he began to include Josh in his next projected development there in Fountain, called Liberty Hills. He had drawn up the streets for his subdivision and named them after Josh. We had to sign permission for Josh's name to be used and then it was sent to the state government for approval of the street names. The design was very special to us. There is one main street that goes by all of the houses in the subdivision with a cul-de-sac at each end. In order to get to that street, "Josh Byers Way," there are only two streets that connect to the highway. They are fittingly named "Hero Lane" and "Honor Lane." It is now a living reality there with all the houses completed and a beautiful community formed. Mary and I were blessed to visit this past summer and see it finished for the first time. I have tried to convince the owners to make a donation of one of the houses to us, so we could live on that street, it hasn't happened. (And, I say this with humor). How wonderful would it be for my home address to be "Josh Byers Way?"

A few days before Josh left for Iraq we talked on the phone, and I had expressed concern for him. I even made the statement that maybe he should have gone in a direction other than the army. Some of the last words he shared with me were, "Dad, I will be just as safe over there in a war zone with bombs dropping all around me if I am in God's will as I would be lying on the beach somewhere sipping lemonade." I had to agree. He was right on target, as always.

It is my prayer that you, the reader, and myself take heed from Josh's instructions. "Keep moving forward." That's what heroes do...

"The credit belongs to the man who is actually in the arena, whose face is marred by dust and sweat and blood, who strives valiantly, who errs and comes short again and again, who knows the great enthusiasms, the great devotions, and spends himself in a worthy cause; who at the best, knows the triumph of high achievement; and who, at the worst, if he fails, at least fails while daring greatly, so that his place shall never be with those cold and timid souls who know neither victory nor defeat." - Theodore Roosevelt

EPILOGUE

by
Mary Byers

Wow! This has been quite a journey. It has been seven years since Josh's death though it seems like yesterday in many ways. There have been a lot of ups and downs, questions and confirmations. Through it all we have learned and we have grown closer to God as a family. I look back now and see that my life is divided between, "before Josh died," and "after Josh died." The loss of a child definitely changes your perspective on life in many ways.

I have watched Lloyd wrestle with beginning to write this book over a period of time and there have been many sleepless nights and anxious days over these past three years since he committed to do this. Josh had always wanted to someday write a book and spoke of that often. He would have done that for sure if he were still alive. That, along with letting others hear his story, brought this modest book to fruition.

If only ten people read these words, it will have still been a success because it has helped us deal with and look closer at our lives and our beliefs.

Someday, we hope to walk on the ground in Iraq where Josh walked and served. We want to stand where he took his last breath. To some that seems morbid, even crazy, but to us it seems healing. I have talked to many Vietnam era Gold Star Mothers who got the opportunity to travel to Vietnam years later and see the place where their sons and daughters fought and died. It was healing for them. My prayer is that God will allow us that privilege someday if we tarry on this earth. I have been told already that Iraq is a very different place from what it was the day Josh died and that it is still improving. Let us hope and pray for peace in that country and elsewhere that violence is thriving.

Knowing Josh as we did, we are certain he laid in bed many nights thinking about how to best lead his men, even at West Point this was constantly on his mind. It is my belief he had consciously made the decision to keep going no matter what if something catastrophic happened to him. His last words are a testimony to that. Thinking of others — not of himself.

"Keep moving forward, Sergeant!"

ACKNOWLEDGEMENTS

In telling about Josh's life, I have been blessed with dedicated servants of God who have given of themselves, their professionalism, and expertise, but mostly out of their love for our Savior and our family.

There are so many who have helped to make this project a reality that it would be impossible to name them all individually.

I do want to personally express my heartfelt thanks to Pat Phillips, who donated her precious time to edit this writing. I felt like I was back in school when I got the manuscript back with red marks here and there. I know it wasn't easy to go home from doing your editor's job all day and have to look at my pitiful writing effort. Mary and I are also grateful for the time our daughter-in-love, Ashley, spent in giving everything a final look.

God also blessed us with the bonds of friendship with Josh's friends, fellow soldiers, who contributed their love for their fellow man by having the courage to open up and share some of the most painful times in their lives.

Every American, whether they acknowledge it or not, owes an eternal gratitude to those men and women who have given their lives to protect our freedom. These heroic soldiers, many who have returned home to live with the horrors of the aftermath of war, are the very backbone of this great country.

Listed below are the names of those who have given $75 or more to help with the publishing costs of this book. We appreciate all the support and love from our friends who have helped make this a reality.

David and Billie Crump
General and Mrs. Charles C. Campbell
David and Elaine Irvin

Mr. and Mrs. Bobby Lindsey
Milton and Mary Virginia Keathley
Grace Efurd
Rick and Diane Higginbotham
Dean and Lisa Lockhart
Sandra Bell
Adult Four Sunday School Class (Trinity)
Lew and Jo Kidd
Gaye and Bud Durham
Burton and Ann Zimmerle
Scottie Fleming
Ray Hill
Ed and Judy Pregel
Gordon and Jesse Jobe
Tom and Gerri Sue Fish
Lloyd and Wilma Pearson
Bobbie Shankle
Harold and Charlotte Frakes
Mrs. Kitty Haddon
Mrs. Ola Buchanan
Jack and Linda Haddock
Paul and Rhonda Sizemore
Donnie and Kathy Huff
Beulah Baptist Church
Providence Presbyterian Church

Due to having to get this information to the publisher by a certain time, we apologize if you gave a gift of $75 or more and were not listed.

CPSIA information can be obtained at www.ICGtesting.com
Printed in the USA
235652LV00002B/2/P

9 781449 716295